T0128768

*Running Through Life*

# Running Through Life

## Barry Worrall

authorHOUSE®

AuthorHouse™
1663 Liberty Drive
Bloomington, IN 47403
www.authorhouse.com
Phone: 1-800-839-8640

First published by AuthorHouse    01/05/2012

ISBN: 978-1-4678-7941-5 (sc)
ISBN: 978-1-4678-7942-2 (ebk)

# LIST OF CONTENTS

# FOREWORD

I wonder if you have ever sat watching one of those "This Is Your Life" programmes on TV. When the celebrity has been mentioned you sit, and look, and you think, "Who the heck is that? I've never heard of him." Perhaps the same could be said for Barry Worrall! Barry Worrall who . . . . ?" Fitness Coach and Consultant. Many might then say, "I'm still none the wiser." But that would be their loss because at one time he was thought to be one of the few completely self-employed Athletics Coach outside the British Athletics Federation (B.A.F.) coaching structure. In an article in the "Northwest Evening Mail" on Tuesday 16 June 1992, three key phrases are used to describe this man extraordinaire. Ability—Guts—Faith in Himself.

Let use those three phrases again; Ability, Guts and Faith in Himself. These are characteristics which help form the backbone and then begin to be the powerhouse that is behind the ability that is Barry Worrall. Perhaps out of these three qualities it is the faith in himself that proved the main staying power in his life. Certainly this is evident when this in-built discipline of staying power sees him through industrial takeovers, redundancies and of sending off job after job applications (37 applications, 30 turndowns). To my mind many people would have in fact thrown in the towel. But you see, the thing about Barry Worrall is this. When the going gets tough, the tough get going!

And so at the age of age of 57 he threw caution to the winds and hit the road as a freelance Athletics coach. In this respect it has to be said that things were still far from easy. Barry wrote to 30 independent schools in Cumbria and north Lancashire without even getting a reply. However his magazine advertisement gave him 14 replies; seven of these were to be new clients. Barry Worrall was indeed running again. Perhaps this is why he is so skilled in urging athletes to continue when they feel it is beyond their power to do so. Barry, you see has mastered this in his industrial life and now teaches people to do the same in the field of Athletics; people like Pat Miller of Barrow in Furness, sixth steeplechaser over 2km in the country, Rob Doyle of Ulverston, and Peter Willacy, also of Barrow. Perhaps here I can mention my own name, Peter Baker. Barry took me from an average club runner (2 minutes for 800 metres) to winning the Sussex 800 metres in a record time and representing British Police (eventually reducing my time to 1 minute 52.2 seconds).

These are not just stories, which are told at the Bay Horse (Barry's local). These are achievements, for Barry gives people the opportunity of seeing beyond their weaknesses. He gives them stamina. He builds up maximum efficiency in running from what he calls technical inefficiency (arms flailing across the body, impairing direction and stance, etc). It is this sort of commitment, from this highly dedicated man, that makes his training regime one of the best, at least for me.

In ending this foreword, not just for a coach, not just to someone who encourages and pushes, but to a friend, for over the years he has become a friend to me—a logical, organised friend and I would like nothing more than to turn on the TV and instead of seeing all those armchair critics and armchair professionals, to see his T shirt bearing his distinctive motif being worn at international level. To end, then! Barry said it was a gamble and he said that he could fail in this venture, because nothing in life is certain. But, as he also said, at the end of an Industrial career, at 57 years of age, at least he is doing something that he enjoys (and is extremely good at), thrives on and so gives back to those athletes who come to him.

Thank you, Barry (or you would say) "For what it's worth." And "What the Hell!"

Peter Baker, Hove, 1994

# CHAPTER 1

# LIFE IS JUST A LOTTERY

In life a lot happens, often at the same time and a truism is "If you want something done, give it to a busy man". This story is about one man's approach to life, a man who worked hard at his job and who was a competitive athlete, and who suffered many periods of unemployment. The same experiences will apply to many people, to women as well as to men. In the UK there has been for many years a strong sporting tradition of personal involvement in physical activity at the professional and amateur level and many people enjoy intense physical activity, which coexists with their professional or working lives. Some follow a professional sporting career while others earn their livings in every type of work.

This book is a personal account of the world of a male club runner, who competed regularly for his Athletics club in what is called "Grass Roots" Athletics. It is a world unknown to most people, but there will be understanding nods of agreement from many people who have competed in other sports. I wasn't a star and remained a club runner and I did my best. My race times were towards the bottom of that ladder which leads from complete obscurity towards mid-range mediocrity. But nowadays my times would take me much further up that ladder, if only because of the lowering of standards as time has passed. For me the five-minute mile, to run 10 miles in the hour and then to beat four minutes forty seconds for the mile on a cinder track, were major performance barriers and then the three hour marathon, each of which I achieved after a lot of effort. I feel that my experiences will strike a chord with many people who experience similar situations, particularly with regard to the mishaps, camaraderie, the humour, which I suspect will exist across all sports and probably across much of life itself. They will relate wholeheartedly to the laughs, tears, the incidents, the potential hazards and the solutions.

Probably the two most appropriate expressions which define human existence are:

"There's nowt so queer as folk." and "Each of us is a prisoner of our own history." The first of these sayings comes from the North of England and is succinct, being composed of six single syllable words and is in my opinion, absolutely true. The second comes directly from my own observations and thought processes; although it is so fundamental that someone must have said it first. There are of course many such sayings throughout the ages, which are not dependent on religious belief, technology, social status, nationality or historical epoch. They stem directly from human experience.

Another two fundamental truths are firstly "The road to hell is paved with good intentions" and secondly that "Most people seek to maximise benefit to him/herself." The first of these usually manifests itself in the legislation passed by our politicians with our best interests at heart (and of course their own) but assume always that all they need to do is to pass a law and that there will exist adequate financial and technical resources needed for their legislation to be successful. But they don't check and don't think their ideas through and disaster beckons for many people. The second of these truths is seen often in the failure of political projects to reach fruition because someone did not get the appropriate benefit or recognition or other people were paid more than he was.

Nothing in life causes as much trouble as money, especially for those who have little, or don't earn much anyway, or those who think they are worth more. Everybody spends money and consequently everyone obtains money. Some are paid from employment, some steal money, some beg for it, some inherit it. Most people go to work to pay their bills, to bring up their family, and to fund their hobbies, sporting, academic, horticultural, etc. They reach their limit in terms of promotion well before they reach middle age and many accept that further promotion is not for them, and their sport or hobbies dominate their thinking for most of their lives. An active sporting interest can be a lifeline to self-respect and sanity, as it was in my case. The office or factory can often be a place of shattered dreams of promotion because of restraints imposed on freedom of action by company practices, by human nature and often viciousness or incompetence of managers. I believe that the most over-used word used nowadays is "Stress", which is blamed for so much, but which is one of life's fundamental and necessary forces. It is possible to combat stress in one area of life with stress in another, totally separated area, in accordance with the truism "A change is as good as a rest." Many aggressive people do not realise that the most powerful and effective words in obtaining results or cooperation from people are "Please" and "Thank you", especially if delivered with a smile.

The sports pages of newspapers and much of the rest of the media bear witness to the many sports clubs and people participating in sport as competitor, official, fan or spectator. I have always enjoyed sport, primarily as a competitive athlete or player, but also as coach, official or spectator and have followed regularly the fortunes of our national teams on TV. "Running" plays a major part in most sports and I have often criticised player performances because so few of them were taught to run efficiently, particularly when they were young. It is noticeable that in much professional sport, many people are obviously overweight, cannot move easily, cannot speak eloquently, but remain earning large salaries because of their one-time high skill levels. My attitude may well be interpreted by my readers as sour grapes on my part and they may be right. After trying football, cricket and rugby, I settled on Athletics as my major competitive sport. However I accept that many people find physical application of the body distasteful and they find different hobbies and interests.

A German bomb on the house next to ours in Hull at the beginning of the war resulted in my being evacuated, along with my older brother and younger sister to Burnley, Lancashire in 1940 where I stayed until I was ten. Then we moved south to Reading in Berkshire, where my father obtained a job as a chef. After schooling I joined the Royal Air Force for my National Service and was posted to Germany, where I started to run in 1954 when I was 19. My main motivation was to get off the camp for the weekend because most of our competition was on other R.A.F or army bases in Germany. I have run ever since. At the time of writing (October 2011) I am 76 years old (77 next month) and run regularly, hence the title of this book. Within the last few years I have been asked if I am running or walking, probably because I have a bad left knee, a very bad right knee and an arthritic toe in my left foot. I benefit from getting out running and building up a sweat and use pedestrians as pace makers and try to match my leg speed to theirs, just to put that little extra pressure onto myself. Old habits die hard and I conform to the saying "Old runners never die; they just get slower." In the 1970's, when it was obvious that I was slowing down, I started to coach runners and have been fortunate to be associated with many athletes, helping them to run faster and have been gratified with the results obtained, not only in improvements in performance, but in friendships made. I qualified as a Senior Coach for the running events from 800 to 10,000 metres with the Amateur Athletic Association (A.A.A.) and later included the steeplechase within my coaching repertoire. With the passing of time, probably like so many of my contemporaries, I feel that my coaching beliefs and practices are not compatible with the prevailing politically correct and Health and Safety regimes together with the tendency towards litigation if things don't go in accordance with what the parent or athlete thinks is right.

At every stage of life each of us faced with choices to make, different ways to go. As we pass through the formal education process we are taught by the teachers who are there at the time. At the age of eleven I won a scholarship to a grammar school and believe that I had a very good education. I remember with affection some of my teachers and shudder at the memory of others. Then the lotteries start, such as why I was good at maths, why I loved gardening and flowers and reading and playing about with words. You hear about people who know from an early age what they want to do and they do it. From my earliest years I wanted to be a pilot, but was rejected by the Royal Air Force selection process, which offered me a career as a navigator. I was not interested in this and on my eighteenth birthday joined the R.A.F. for three years for my National Service and trained as an Air Wireless Mechanic.

I have been fortunate in that I became involved in a sport to which I was suited and which I have continued throughout my adult life, namely "Athletics" and specifically "Running". I tried other sports and in my teens I was a goalkeeper for a village football team in Berkshire and played cricket, again for a village team, but without demonstrating any serious ability. In Athletics I liked the fact that you have to work hard just to remain at the same level. Running is an all-round activity, track in summer, cross-country in winter and road running throughout the year. In my early running years I felt extreme chest discomfort while running, because of the breathing exertions and thought that I had breathing or other problems. However, when competing in the London to Brighton road relay for Reading Athletic Club in the early sixties I saw well known international athletes running very hard and at the extreme painful edge of their capabilities, breathing very hard and noisily and desperately trying to catch the man in front. I realised that most runners experienced the same discomfort and I was not at fault. This was my "Welcome to Running" and from that time my training and racing took on a new dimension and I was hooked. I became a runner. I learned to do what all runners do, to work harder and harder and I have not stopped.

In the 1960's while competing for Queens Park Harriers and then Reading Athletic Club, I spent some years enjoying ballroom dancing, and joined the South London Judo Club where I obtained an orange belt in judo. In addition I have always enjoyed good quality, argumentative and witty conversation and have followed the ale trail wherever I found it.

Major activities for us all are studying for an educational qualification, learning skills for a trade or profession, just to earn a living. We often have intense political or religious beliefs and then of course there is our emotional existence, finding one's life-long soul mate, etc and these forces shape the directions of our lives for the long term. Other influences are our likes and dislikes, passions or emotions and of course those things which just go wrong. Sometimes an apparently minor incident can dominate your thought processes for a long time and can have a major change of direction in your life. And then we have the other side of life, namely our hobbies or the physical part of life, namely do we play sport, or dance. Are we gripped by a particular person, sport or pastime, which absorbs us night and day? All these considerations coexist and are dealt with by most people and somehow we survive, depending on our individual ability to sort things out to our own advantage.

On returning to Civvy Street from National Service at the end of 1955 I tried to work out what I wanted to do for the rest of my life, but like so many youngsters, just did not know; I was restless and wanted a career offering excitement. In February 1956, after four months labouring on building sites I joined the Metropolitan Police, trained at Peel House, just off Vauxhall Bridge Road and I was lucky enough to be posted to Paddington Green Police Station, a marvellous training ground in application of policing principles. In August 1956, while still a very raw rookie constable, I had booked into the police section house for an official tea break and I was involved in an incident which pushed me further on my journey into Athletics and this is related in "Stolen Hats—An Introduction to Athletics" in Chapter 3. After nearly four years, once again I was restless and realised that I needed more out of life, so I enrolled on an evening course for GCE Advanced Level Mathematics at Regent Street Polytechnic. The ease with which I accepted the studying convinced me that I needed to change direction. One day when I was at home on my day off I was cycling past Reading University in Whiteknights Park in Reading and on a whim, turned into the entrance, along a long drive past the playing fields and went into the Physics Department where I met the Head of Department and asked for a job. Some weeks later I was offered a post as a Laboratory Technician and for the next four years studied at Reading and then Farnborough Technical Colleges, and ended up with a Higher National Certificate (HNC) in Radio Communications.

My industrial future was established and I became an Electrical Engineer, much of my working life being spent in the Defence and Process Control industries. My constant and faithful companion throughout has been my love of running and after a career as a mid-range club level athlete with a number of Athletic clubs I qualified as a running coach. In this way I have maintained my contact with running and runners and think it has been time well-spent. I am proud to call myself simply "A Runner". The benefits of running were evident for me when I was able to maintain concentration until the end of exhausting days. However, in all probability, my fitness and attitude probably made me belligerent and awkward to some of my colleagues.

A constant theme in life is that things go wrong, usually at an inconvenient time and this often forces changes in one's intentions, a situation rcognised by Robbie Burns when he stated "The best laid schemes o' mice an' men gang aft a-gley." One example of this phenomenon occurs with the wearing of false teeth (dentures), which many people wear and most of the time they work well. But it is certain that the denture will break at some (inconvenient) moment. Then comes the realisation that you have to get it repaired quickly, because you have an important meeting the next day, so you have to do something. Another feature of false teeth is that in playing some sports it is recommended that you take them out because you might swallow them while involved in your sport. But where do you put them for the duration of your sporting activity? More importantly, do you remember where you put them for safekeeping? Sometimes you win back the situation, sometimes you don't.

Then there is the short-term memory syndrome, where you go out of the office but just outside the door you pause and say to yourself, "What have I come out here for?" This happened to me when I was in my early thirties and I made the mistake of voicing my thoughts out loud, just as a colleague was walking past me in the corridor. He looked at me quizzically, frowned, paused, was about to say something, but then thought better of it and walked by. This story raises smiles when I tell it and it obviously touches a chord in many people. I explain then that this memory loss was caused by my thinking quickly of many things and is not because I am getting older, although that of course can accentuate the problem. It is amazing how a screwdriver or pen can drop onto the floor, bounce and then disappear from view, not to be found without extensive search and sometimes not even then. We deal with many crises regularly and each one has the potential to exert a major change in life's direction. In my case a chance conversation with an athlete after a coaching session resulted in my moving from Sussex to Cumbria in 1987: for details see "Coaching Runners for Athletics and Other Sports" in Chapter 12.

I pursued an engineering career, which took years of study and did not lead to riches. At best a comfortable lifestyle was all that could realistically be achieved. Runners, both men and women, are intense about their sport and at times, with races coming up, they often devote more nervous and intellectual energy to running than about their profession. However they train at high intensity and often hold down a demanding job, bring up a family, do the household chores, gardening, car-maintenance, and just getting on with family life. In the sixties many such athletes were able to achieve high performances for Great Britain in Olympics and major championships while working very hard daily at their job or profession. In 2011 the majority of international athletes expect to obtain funding from some benevolent organisation and are aggrieved when they no longer receive their (lottery) funding, because their performances are not of the required standard. Tough!

In the Olympics Athletics framework most of the events are running events, from the 100-metre sprint to the marathon. The marathon commemorates the feat of the Greek soldier Pheidippides who in 490BC ran from Marathon to Athens in Greece to bring news of the Greek victory in battle over the Persians. In the1908 Olympic Games in London, the marathon distance was changed to 26 miles to cover the distance from Windsor Castle to White City stadium, and a further

385 yards was added so that the race could finish in front of the royal box containing King Edward VII and other dignitaries. After much subsequent discussion the official marathon distance was established for the 1924 Olympic Games in Paris as 42.195 km or 26 miles 395 yards.

In many circles and in this book, running implies the endurance events, namely from 800 metres upwards. The track finals in the Olympic Games are held in the main Olympic arena and the watching millions often become intensely involved in and have applauded absorbing races. At the time of writing thoughts of many of our politicians, media and athletes will be focused on the London Olympic Games in 2012 and I personally am pessimistic about the chances of British runners even to reach the quarter finals, because of what I see as neglect on the part of our Sport's leaders over many years. However miracles might happen.

Running is a fundamental human activity, which is applied in most team sports and also recreationally and for health reasons. Anyone who wants to run can join an athletic club and find races on road, country or track and many have done so, and have developed a life-long passion. I see many people out running but rarely see a "real runner", i.e. who is running obviously in the discomfort zone, which many runners in the past entered regularly. But I welcome the mass participation events, such as 10k's to marathons if only because the training which each of the competitors does will improve his/her cardio-vascular system and will reduce the frequency of their visits to the doctors' surgeries. It may even be the way to tackle obesity, the future major killer in western society.

Most runners are amateurs, but intensely professional in application, driven by the desire to improve and to beat the athlete in front. They earn their living in every type of job and train and race in their spare time. Some try to earn a living from running, but few succeed. The introduction of money prizes and rewards has not changed the desire to win, which is primeval in origin, but has, in my opinion, changed the athletes' focus and has resulted in them running slower, particularly in the western world. As has been stated, running is boring, but once past a certain point it becomes an aim in itself and then becomes an integral part of the runner's daily life. It co-exists with work, family and the usual ups and downs of life. Media attention is invariably focussed onto the high level performers, but the same intensity competitions are held regularly every weekend, particularly in the UK, but obviously at much lower performance levels. This book relates how one runner lived his life during a period which many people would regard as stressful, but which is just part of life. Each day, whatever happens, is just another day. He has learned to live his life in compartments in each of which he drives himself far harder than he drives anyone else.

This runner is a loner, competitive and single-minded. He is scathing in assessing other runners and at times sees more of his running mates than his family. When running with other athletes, conversation is mostly about running and he does not know (or care about) what his club mates do for a living, their hobbies other than running, or about their religion. He sometimes runs in a group, but is used to running on his own. He is invariably disappointed in his own performances because he sets unrealistic targets, regardless of his prevailing fitness level. He finds peace of mind and relaxation when running and invariably feels good after finishing. While running, his mind free wheels and he turns over problems in his mind, often solving a problem whose solution has until then eluded him. He races as often as his family life allows, and refuses to accept that he must slow down with increasing age. He just loves to run and is never happier than when he is out pounding the roads, pavements or (in daylight) on grass or forests. Once a week, after 9pm when the children are in bed, he is allowed out to the pub with his running friends, where they spend the time drinking beer and talking, not surprisingly, about Athletics and specifically, "Running."

In my Engineering life I was made redundant several times (from 1983 to 1987 I had five redundancies and a sixth in 1991). I continued to train throughout these periods and use these experiences to set the scene for my first story, "Just Another Day—Unemployed or Just Between Jobs," in Chapter 2, which describes the process of training for a marathon while unemployed and looking for a job. The subsequent chapters relate other anecdotes from the world of "Running." I completed five marathons and dropped out of one, this latter being described in painful detail in chapter 4, "Athletics Folklore". In this book I include details of three marathons in all, my first being the Boston Marathon in 1970 when I was 36, the Maxol Marathon in 1973, aged 39, when I broke 3 hours for the first time, and my fastest time of 2 hours 52 minutes 59 seconds being set in the Harlow Marathon in 1974, which provides the inspiration for Chapter 2.

It has been my constant habit to write about events soon after taking part in them and this provides an element of immediacy and time-frame relevance on some aspects of the sport, particularly with regard to the stories and anecdotes. I hope that this brief snapshot of what in some ways are bygone ages will amuse my readers and will also be relevant to anyone who just "Goes out for a run."

Finally a few words about the format of this book are needed. Probably the most popular race in the mind of the public is the marathon, 42.2 kilometres or 26 miles 365 yards and I completed five such races before I entered the first London marathon in 1981, when I was 46, hoping to run a personal best (pb) time. Alas, six weeks before the race a very good friend of mine, over a pint on one of our Thursday night drinking sessions said, "Oh, Barry will be all right. He never gets injured." Two weeks later, on a long run I hobbled home with a back injury and did not run another marathon, despite spending many hours undergoing physiotherapy and osteopathic treatment. However I have continued to run shorter distances and qualified as a running coach so have retained my contact with athletes and the Sport.

This book starts with "Unemployed or Just Between Jobs," a typical story of a six month period in which a middle-aged man with a wife and two young children was made redundant, searched for work and finally obtained another job, but over the same period continuing trained for a marathon, in which he set his best time. Hopefully it will interest and amuse the reader in the turbulent times which existed then and which lie ahead.

I am regularly reminded of a comment by my manager in the USA in 1970 when we were assembled for a meeting at short notice, because of possible bomb threats throughout the company. He came into the room, looked at us and said, "Gentlemen, we are living in troubled times." Things have not changed.

# CHAPTER 2

# JUST ANOTHER DAY—UNEMPLOYED OR JUST BETWEEN JOBS

## List of Contents

## 1. Synopsis

This story is typical about a middle-aged man whose main passion outside work and family is "Running". The story relates how, after being made redundant, he combines job interviews, with training for a marathon, the race itself, while at he same time dealing with normal household and family activities. Names of persons and companies are fictitious and any resemblance to any person, living or dead, is purely coincidental.

On arriving home after work he receives a telephone call asking him to attend an interview for another job. He has been redundant before and the warning signals in his present company have suggested that he may be made redundant again. He has been actively looking for another job for some time.

He is apolitical, well read, up-to-date with current affairs, and immerses himself totally in his job, which he enjoys. He is highly motivated and intense about his work in the Commercial Department of a large Engineering company. Because of his single-minded and competitive approach he can appear impatient for results and he tends to speak before considering the consequences, a habit which has made enemies and his managers uneasy about promoting him.

He is devoted to his wife and family and is closely involved in bringing up his two young sons. He and his wife have always maintained the sanctity of their family unit and to that end one of them has always been available to the children. She has reluctantly accepted his running habits and manages the home ruthlessly efficiently on their income, which is never enough, and makes sure that his running does not interfere with the lives of the children, although she accepts that he does his fair share in their upbringing. He and his wife are usually in bed before 10pm because of the need to be up early in the morning to attend to one or other of the children. Their constant joke is, "We won't watch the film on TV tonight because we'll be able to see it when the kids are grown up."

A runner often has a busy life outside his sport and he fits in his daily runs whenever he can, sometimes running home from work but then having to solve the logistics problem of having clothing in the correct place for the next phase of his daily life. He searches his days and finds new pockets of time, such as early mornings, lunchtimes and evenings to enable him to train without interfering with the normal day. He is often reminded of a Dutch Engineering Project Leader whose favourite saying was, "You have 24 hours a day and the nights as well." which illustrates an attitude of mind. When the runner travels on business the first thing into the suitcase is his running gear and in a strange city he often runs from the hotel, turning left, left again and left again until he gets back to the hotel. This system generally works well but every so often it doesn't and this can lead to frenzied questioning of local inhabitants about the location of the hotel.

Running is a simple fundamental activity, having been practised by mankind since the world began. It forms the basis of most sports using a ball, e.g. football, rugby, hockey, lacrosse, cricket and can have serious application in fitness preparation for other ball games such as golf, tennis and table tennis. Practitioners of these other sports usually dislike, or detest, running, purely because it is so boring. They prefer, quite naturally, to spend their time doing the things they like doing, namely kicking, throwing, hitting the ball etc. From ancient Greek times the simple foot race, man against man, woman against woman, has stimulated the applause and recriminations of the watching audiences, dependent on their affiliations and interests. Within the last 150 to 200 years running has developed as a sport in its own right and in the 20th Century coalesced into the Olympic movement, despite the interruptions of two world wars.

His wife complains that his hair is too long and he decides to have it cut very short in an attempt to increase speed in the next big race and is subjected to good-natured banter from his work colleagues, to which he caustically reacts and returns home to his wife's reaction. Immediately afterwards he is made redundant and applies himself to find another job, while at the same time trying to maintain family life and training for a marathon later in the year. Please read on.

## **2. Get Your Hair Cut**

Peter heard the phone ringing as he inserted the key in the Yale lock of his front door. It rang for the fourth time as he picked up the receiver from the hall table.

"Hello, Peter Sharpe, good afternoon."

A pleasant well-modulated, soft and seductive, woman's "come-to-bed" voice said, "Could I speak to Mr. Brian Sharpe, please?" He bet she smelled nice. This had to be an official call. Since he could remember he had always been called Peter in the home and did not realise until he was called up into the armed services that on his birth certificate his names were shown as "Brian Denis

Peter". He learned later that his dad was abroad in the Merchant Navy when he was christened and an uncle had given the names to the vicar at the christening, but had got them in the wrong order. Since being made aware of this Peter had used the name "Brian" only on all forms and official documentation.

"Speaking," he replied.

"Hello Mr. Sharpe. Jenny Davidson, Henderson Systems, speaking. It's about your letter for our Test Engineer position. Ian Morris, our Group Personnel Manager, would like to talk to you. Sorry about the short notice, but he would like to get this done in the next few days if possible. He has little free time within the next few weeks and asked me to contact you to try to arrange an interview as soon as possible."

"Just hold on please, while I get my diary," he replied, trying to sound nonchalant. He had to appear hard to get, although there was nothing shown in there for the next week. "Right—what time is suitable for you? I can manage Thursday, that's tomorrow, or Friday afternoon of this week." They arranged an appointment for 2pm on the Friday, the earliest mutually agreeable time, although he shuddered. The interviewer would be thinking of the weekend and would want to get the interview over as quick, because it was Friday. He would have to battle with the rush hour traffic, always horrendous on Fridays.

He put the phone down onto its cradle, paused, and took off his coat, which he hung on a hook on the coat stand. He glanced down at the long white envelope on the carpet immediately below the letter flap. The letter was thin and must have contained only one A4 page, because it was almost certainly a 'No' letter. He knew immediately what it said without opening it. These rejection letters always used the same three sentences, "Thanks for applying for the job. We regret to inform you that you have not been successful. We will keep your details on file." He picked it up and put it on the hall table, to be looked at and filed later.

Babs was out, probably shopping, and the children were not back yet because of their games after school. The house was quiet and the late afternoon sun shone through the windows, etching in sharp relief on the wall the borders and delicate spiders-web designs of the lace curtains. It had been a brutal day. He could feel the tension in his shoulders and still smarted from the tongue lashing at work that afternoon. His head ached, not the hangover-ache, but a dull ache resulting from the permanent fear-driven atmosphere in the Commercial Department where everybody was wondering who would be next for the chop, that request to go into the manager's office or to the Personnel Department.

He needed a run—that would help. He went upstairs, changed into shorts and T-shirt and came downstairs in bare feet and into the garage for his running shoes. They were kept there because Babs complained regularly and bitterly about "that revolting smell." When out running he did not wear socks and for years had rubbed petroleum jelly over his feet before each run. The shoe soon acquired a powerful pungent odour, of rotten meat, and probable decay of the particular plastics used in their manufacture. The smell of his trainers had caused much caustic comment, and had once emptied a men's changing room. However, Babs had often remarked that the skin on his feet was in excellent condition so maybe he was doing something right. He stuck his nose into one shoe. "Just marginally ripe", he thought and sat down on a stool to put them on. He paused in the kitchen to scribble a note for Babs "Out for run, back 6 o'clock." He touched his waistband, to make sure that he had the house keys. They were held on a key ring through which he passed his handkerchief and this was slipped inside the elastic waistband of his shorts. He went out of the front door, closed the door behind him, and waited to hear the snick of the Yale lock as the door closed.

He jogged out of the drive, turned left onto the pavement, which was separated from the kerb by a grass verge in which were planted flowering cherry trees whose tops formed a pulsating canopy of pink blossom all the way down the road. On the left he could see the long row of red brick bungalows and semi-detached houses, built in the fifties and sixties. He turned left towards the footpath into the park and set off slowly, waiting for the stiffness to disappear.

"Afternoon Harry," he said to his neighbour, who was casually raking his front lawn and ran straight ahead before he could be expected to stop and talk. He started the run, the aches in his knees and shoulders gradually easing as he warmed up. He passed the door of the saloon bar of the Red Lion pub, one of his locals (and also his one mile check point) in just outside six and a half minutes and started to relax. He turned into the park and his breathing became gentler and quieter as he relaxed and then louder as pushed himself harder and suddenly he felt himself sprinting on the shallow downhill. The second mile checkpoint (the large oak tree by the lake) passed by in 12 minutes. "Absolutely flying now. I can't keep this up," he thought, "I've got to save something for the big race. "Oh, what the hell," he said to himself, "It feels too good to stop now."

He turned into the forest and relaxed before running down the slope through the trees, his favourite section. As he ran he felt the tension dropping away and he pushed himself harder. He ran out of the trees and turned right for the last long run down the hill back to his road, turned on his customary finishing burst for the benefit of any curious onlookers (none seen there so far) and finished in his drive. Then he leaned on the house wall for support. His chest was heaving, the sweat was dripping off his forehead, down his cheeks and chin and onto the tarmac drive. He could feel his wet cotton T-shirt clinging to his shoulders. He leaned down to remove his running shoes. Then, in bare feet and carrying his running shoes in his hand, he walked over the hot sun-drenched concrete onto the cooler shaded portion slowly to the back door.

The door opened, and out came Babs, "Oh, hello, Peter," she said, nearly hitting him with the large white plastic shopping bag she was taking out to the bin just outside the door. "You were home early. Have a good run?" Without waiting for an answer she said, "Make sure you put those smelly shoes in the garage, not in the kitchen." He sighed—back to reality. "Oh, while you are at it," she added, "when are you going to get your haircut. It's a mess, flopping around all the time." Maybe one of the boys had upset her.

He took off his trainers, put them in the garage, just by the open window and went upstairs into the bathroom for a quick shower. Feeling relaxed and more at ease with the world he dressed in the bedroom and made his way down the stairs.

His thoughts returned to the telephone call and to the letter. He opened it and, as suspected, the letter was another "No." He had received three in the last week and every one still hurt even though his first redundancy had occurred three years previously. He reached for the bulky "Job Applications" box file in which he kept all job adverts and correspondence on every job he had applied for. He filed the letter with its paperwork and pulled out the file relating to the job the lady had talked about on the phone. As he read he remembered that the advert had appeared twice. He had applied after the first advert but had received a "No" letter. They must have had second thoughts to ask him in again.

He and Babs sat on the settee in the front room. He stroked her hair, "Cup of tea?" he asked. She nodded. When seated comfortably on the settee they talked about the threatening atmosphere at work; each worried about the grim prospect of his being out of work. But there was the new job interview—and new hope, which he had learned always springs eternal.

Outside work, the Harlow Marathon in late October had been occupying his dreams and thoughts for months. He desperately wanted to run a personal best (pb) for this race and his best time of 2h 59m 32s was now four years old. The marathon requires the athlete to be on his feet continuously for two to four hours, far longer than he is normally on his feet in the working day. The marathon distance is 42.2 kilometres (26.2 miles) and requires a lot of running in training, 70 miles a week being the norm for international standard athletes capable of running each mile in five minutes which results in a time of 2 hours 11 minutes. At this level the athlete will be training for about twelve hours per week or over 90 minutes per day, assuming he runs every day. If preparation time for each run is considered, it can be seen that the elite marathon runner needs well over two hours per day for changing, training, and showering. Peter's mileages and available time for training were much less.

Most runners love just to go out for a run, usually alone, but occasionally with one or more companions. Marathoners often go out for long runs, which improve cardio-vascular efficiency (use of oxygen), at a pace they can sustain for hours. A standard method of improving running speed is to run a session, in which the athlete runs a known distance, normally 400 metres or multiples of that distance, which he repeats several times, with a rest period in between, known as the recovery. In these sessions running speeds are much higher than in longer runs and by careful choice of the distance, quantity and duration of recovery the runner can improve his running speed dramatically over longer distances. These sessions are often run on running tracks but they can equally well be run on the road or on grass, in parks or in forests. The down side of these sessions is the increased concentration required and discomfort caused.

For a road session Peter would select a half-mile course on road or pavement and confirm the distance by driving round it in the car, or with the Ordnance Survey map. Ideally he would choose a course with no roads on the left hand side for safety reasons and try to have distinctive start and finish points. He would then run the measured distance, first in one direction, then the other, usually six or eight in total, having a rest or recovery between each run of between 90 seconds and three minutes. He calculated the average time, regardless of wind speed or direction.

He used a local park or forest for his off-road session, which was then due. He ran out of the drive, turned left and ran to the large sports field just over a mile from his drive. He turned in through the gates and jogged slowly to the start of one of his accurately measured half-mile runs. He went through his stretching routine, gently working each major joint complex from head to toe, making sure that each joint operated over its normal range, with no restrictions. Then he went through the standard pre-race and pre-session running drills, the standard high knees and "kick your bum" heel flicks used to prepare the legs for faster running.

He walked back to ten metres behind the start line, flexed his legs again, took a deep breath, stepped forward and then accelerated with short strides, pressing the stopwatch start button as he crossed the start line. He kept the pace going for 100 metres before easing back into a more controlled pace. He felt the tension building up in his arms and shoulders but knew that he could control it until the end of the circuit and stopped the watch at the end at 2m 40s.

"Not bad," he thought, and walked along the path past the start before turning round to start the second run, 90 seconds later. In this recovery period he felt his heart rate drop and started the second run with the same intensity as the first. Once again he eased back after 100 metres, slipped into his economical although fast rhythm and the watch showed 2m 34s. The third run took one second less and then times for the next drifted out to 2 minutes 35 and then 2 minutes 40. "This is no good," he snarled "Come on, fool, let's see what you're made of." Aching all over he ran the next one slightly faster and then the penultimate run two seconds faster still. As he approached the start line for the last run sweat was pouring down from his leaking forehead and over his eyeballs, making it difficult for him to see. He grinned inwardly as he recalled that standard runners' expression. It's got to be 'Eyeballs out.'

Peter leapt into the final run and tried to maintain the rhythm as long as possible, driving his arms harder, although beginning to wobble as his finish line appeared. He barely believed the 2 minutes 25 seconds shown on the watch. He leaned against the trunk of the tree by the finish, watched from his vantage point in the oak tree on the other side of the path by a grey squirrel, motionless except for a single twitch of its tail. Peter blinked and the squirrel had disappeared.

He uncoiled himself from the trunk and felt relieved that the session was over. He slowly jogged back along the field to make his way back home and calculated his average time as 2 minutes 34 seconds, his best session for some time and knew that he was fit. He felt that exhilaration which came from finishing a very hard, demanding session, when the heart rate gradually drops, and the jog back home was much smoother than the outward run.

## 3. Haircut and Consequences

The next morning Peter went downstairs, took Babs her cup of tea, just to allow her to wake up slowly, before her own hectic day started. He cooked his breakfast, collected his work papers into his briefcase and went to the door. "Make sure you do something about your hair—it's too long," she uttered. He had arranged to have a few hours off that morning for the haircut and some urgent shopping so he went out of the back door, opened the garage door to wheel out his bicycle, closed the door behind him and cycled down the short drive into the street. He used his bicycle to travel the short journey to work because it was much easier and was cheaper than using the car. He carried his briefcase in his haversack, which he wore up between the shoulder blades, and turned right towards the town instead of left towards the industrial estate where the factory was situated.

He cycled into town, to the reference section of the Public Library, where he looked in the reference manuals for information on Henderson Holdings. They were a large holding company comprising a number of small and medium-sized companies, which designed and manufactured electrical appliances and equipment for military applications and had a number of establishments, their head office being in Camberley. He noted down relevant information about them, the name of their chairman, the previous year's turnover and details about the product range. Their entry contained an article written by their sales director about their products and particularly his enthusiastic view of their future direction. This gave Peter some data, which is always valuable before going in for a job interview. However there was no data there about Henderson Controls, the small company he was going to see.

Feeling more settled, he cycled from the library into the High Street and just after 11 o'clock entered the barber's shop, the now-hot sun making itself felt on the back of his neck. A burly man, wearing a thick lumberjack tartan shirt and heavy work boots, occupied the barber's chair. Over his shoulders was a white towel to protect the jacket from the hair cuttings. Peter sat down on the dark brown wooden bench seat which went all round the room and thumbed through the sports pages of a tabloid newspaper which lay on the bench. After a short wait the man in the chair got up, wiped his neckband with a tissue given to him by the barber, paid him with a smile and then went through the door into the street. Then the barber approached Peter and waved him to the chair. The barber was short, a plump little middle-aged man, dressed in black trousers, highly polished black shoes and a white smock coat, under which he wore a white shirt and a blue tie. He had short stubby fingers and his round clean-shaven smooth face was topped with an incredibly thick mass of black curly hair. He had not cut Peter's hair before, although he had seen him in the shop. Peter knew that his name was Luigi and his accent suggested that he was Italian.

The barber's face creased into a practised smile as he waved Peter towards the large black simulated-leather barber's chair, which he swung round to allow him to climb into it easily. Having sat down Peter took off his spectacles, folded them and put them into his shirt pocket. Luigi swivelled the chair round so that Peter could see himself in the large mirror mounted on the wall above the black pseudo-marble work surface in front of him. From behind the chair he looked into Peter's eyes in the mirror "How do you like it, sir?" he asked, smiling with his lips only, the eyes non-committed.

"I want it short, please," Peter replied, nervously, "I've heard of something called a brush cut."

"I don't think it would suit you, sir," Luigi replied tactfully.

Peter thought for a moment and then said, "I want it very short on top."

Luigi sighed. "Well it's your hair, sir," he replied, "and you are paying for it so you can have what you like." He paused, "How short do you want it, sir, so short?" As he said this he closed his thumb to his first finger, leaving a gap of about an inch.

"No, a bit shorter than that." Peter replied.

"Well, you are paying for it, sir," he replied, pausing before the last word, which was hissed through tightly-pressed lips.

He moved forward around the chair and picked up his clippers from the work surface, paused and then with one practised movement, ran the clippers along Peter's right scalp, cutting a swathe through the hair. He paused, as though to savour his handiwork and then continued cutting backwards and forwards until the sides and back were done to his satisfaction. Peter was aware of the hair cuttings dropping past his eyes like snowflakes passing a window in a snowstorm. Some lodged on his nostril and made it itch, so he blew some air through that nostril to dislodge the hair. It worked. A quick nervous thought flashed through his brain. "What have I done now?" he asked himself.

Luigi put down the clippers, picked up a pair of scissors and reached over to the top of Peter's head. He grasped some hairs in his left hand and lifted them straight up and with a single movement, cut through the bundle, leaving one-inch long strands feebly clutching the air, each strand unable to remain upright under its own weight. He giggled nervously and repeated the action with another bundle. Peter sensed another presence, glanced into the mirror and saw a man in a dark suit, probably the manager, at Luigi's shoulder. The manager stepped forward, put his fingers onto Peter's scalp where Luigi had cut the bunches, faced him, and muttered angrily in his own language. Peter saw Luigi's shoulders inch up in a shrug, heard his defiant though apologetic reply and the manager walked away, shaking his head.

Once again Luigi picked up the clippers and with a few deft strokes reduced the top hair layer to what appeared to be a dust covering and he then went over the back and sides again. When he finished Luigi held up a mirror behind Peter's head. Peter replaced his spectacles on his nose and Luigi swung the mirror from one side to the other, to allow Peter to see both sides of the back of his head. That was all right as far as he could see. Luigi tilted the mirror and moved his body aside. Peter's heart sank as he looked at the reflection in the large mirror. He recognised the face in the mirror but on his scalp almost invisible short hairs formed ridges along the centre of pink and white patches of skin. On each side was the short, clipped appearance of the short back and sides standard military version, which had until then presented his head to the world.

Peter got down from the chair and accepted the tissue held in Luigi's fingertips to wipe away any hair clippings from inside his collar. They walked over to the till by the door and Peter paid him, adding separately the customary tip into his outstretched palm and walked self-consciously out of the shop into the bright sunlight of the busy high street. He felt the immediate cooling effect of the light breeze on his scalp, now about to become pink because it would be exposed to more direct sunlight. Nobody stopped and stared and that was the first hurdle over. Now for work.

To reach his office, which he shared with five other engineers and Bernard Harris, their section boss, Peter had to go through the Accounts Section, which contained about ten typewriters or accounting machines, operated by women of various ages. It was usually bustling and vibrant with noise from the machines and the women chatting. Peter opened the double glass doors and was aware of the usual noises, which suddenly stopped. Each desk was occupied. In the silence he realised that everybody had stopped talking and working and more alarmingly, were all looking at him. After pausing slightly he walked through the office towards the double doors on the opposite wall. As he held out his hand to grab the handle of the door the silence was ended by a long drawn-out wolf whistle from Maggie from her desk just by the door he needed to go through. She was tall and willowy, just under 30, married with two lovely children but often wore skirts short enough to play havoc with male concentration. She had light brown curly hair and that day wore a dark blue cashmere wool sweater and buttock-hugging jeans, her legs perched tantalisingly on dark blue medium height heels.

He paused, pulled the door open and then walked forwards, eyes firmly focused on the outside. He burned inwardly as he felt Maggie's gaze. "Wow!" she uttered, as he was level with her. He made his escape through the door just as the giggles and sighs increased and changed to amused laughter, which was then muffled as the door closed behind him.

Peter walked into his main office, a large rectangular room, well lit by the sun and the blue cloudless sky, which could be seen through the large windows on the right hand wall. He walked towards his desk, to the right of the central aisle, which led to the office of Bernard, their manager. Peter's colleagues were all ex-servicemen from Army and Air Force, and all family men. They occupied the other five desks in that office. Through the open door of Bernard's office Peter could see him in shirtsleeves and tie, sitting behind his desk, looking at Alan and Gordon who sat with their backs to Peter. Bernard was obviously concerned about something, his finger pushing down onto a large engineering drawing, which almost covered his desk. Their heads were all intently focused, looking down and it was obvious that they were totally absorbed in their problem. Peter wondered what the problem was and whether he would be involved. Alan, Gordon and he were working on the same project.

Peter slid into his chair, hoping nobody would notice. "Afternoon all," he uttered, looking down at his desk, automatically sliding his hand to unlock his drawer to obtain his files. But Ian, who occupied the desk in front of him, was much too quick "Been having a haircut in company time Pete?" he asked, grinning.

"No, in my lunchtime, but anyway, it grows in company time." he retorted.

"Not all of it." he said.

"But I didn't have all off." he replied.

Eddie came back from lunch, paused while he took off his topcoat, "Morning Curly," he said, grinning.

"You mean afternoon, don't you," Peter snarled back. "Anyway, I prefer Blondie."

The noise brought Bernard out of the office, closely followed by Gordon and then belatedly by Alan. Bernard Harris was tall, with angular features, invariably wearing a mournful expression and started each day wearing a grey pin-stripe double breasted suit but removed his jacket early on and hung it on the back of his chair. He suffered from an upset stomach and a wife who stated to anyone who would listen that he deserved far more in life than he was achieving. He would leave his shirtsleeves unbuttoned and the cuffs flapped gently as he used his hands to emphasise his comments, which were many—mainly complaining about the work offered to him for comment or approval.

"Get a haircut, did you?" said Gordon, in his Welsh lilt, joining in the baiting.

"A bit short isn't it?" asked Bernard with concern." You'll catch your death of cold, Peter. Why on earth did you do it?"

"It'll help me run faster. "Peter stuttered.

Alan just looked, in some bewilderment. "I tell you what," he said, confidentially as he lowered his voice. "We needed a break, it was getting serious in there," pointing to Bernard's office.

Brian peered through his spectacles at Peter's scalp. "Christ, Pete," he uttered, "Come a bit close to the razor?" Peter just stared at him.

"What made you do it, Pete?" Brian asked.

Bernard said, "If I had a haircut cut like that my wife wouldn't sleep with me—I'd be out on the sofa."

"Listen mate," Peter replied, warming to the battle," All you have to do is tell her, 'Look dear, I'm sleeping here, and you can sleep where you like."

"Pete's got the right idea," said Gordon.

"I couldn't do that," Bernard replied," She'd murder me."

"I wouldn't dare go home with hair like that," said Brian, a note of admiration in his voice.

The rest of the day was spent getting the factory used to the haircut.

"Get a haircut," yelled Eddie from inside a milling machine. Almost rising to the bait Peter said, "Why don't you . . . !" and then stopped as he noticed interested people turning their heads towards us, "You're only jealous," he retorted.

"You've not started meditating, have you Pete?" he asked, grinning.

37

"I've been offered a part in a film as a monk." Peter replied.

People slowly became accustomed to the haircut but there was one final hurdle to overcome that day—Babs. He sometimes wore a cap when on the bike and needed it even more now with reduced natural protection for the head against heat and cold. He cycled into the drive and round to the back of the house. He leaned the bike against the garage wall and opened the side door which led into the kitchen and there was Babs with her back to the door. She heard him come in and turned with a welcoming smile on her face. He paused and then took off his cap. Her smile froze, her bottom lip trembled and then her eyes froze over. He knew the symptoms. She didn't know whether to laugh or cry. "Well you told me to get a hair cut," he replied.

He needed a run and hoped that Babs would have simmered down when he got back. He went upstairs, changed into shorts and T-shirt and came downstairs, to pick up his running shoes from the garage. "Going out for a short run. See you later, Babs," he said, before heading down the drive. As he ran, he felt the cold seeping into his scalp, the obvious effect of the haircut. "I need a cap," he thought so turned back, opened the door and picked up a black baseball cap from the hook behind the door and put it on. "That's better," he thought and jogged down the street, gradually increasing speed as he warmed up. He returned after a hard 45 minutes run, feeling hot, relaxed and very pleased with himself. Maybe the haircut would work.

When the boys were in bed, Peter and Babs sat on the settee in the front room and talked about the situation at work. "Bernard called us in today. This bid we're working on has to be right. If we don't get it right and get the order some of us will go."

"That job you applied for. Have you heard from them?" she asked, concern showing on her face and in her voice.

"Not yet" he replied. "I had the last interview ten days ago. I thought I did well and they wanted me with them, but you know, my measure of the success of an interview. If they don't reply within a fortnight they don't want you. Still we've just got to do the best we can on this bid."

## 4. Redundant

The next morning he was dragged, reluctantly, out of a deep sleep at 5.45am by the harsh clanging of the alarm clock, that "Wake-The-Dead" alarm clock which had belonged to his mother and she had been deaf. It had two copper dome-shaped semi-spheres, of different natural frequencies so that when struck in sequence by the copper striker rod, the echoes of the last four hits on each intermingled and echoed and reached down into the deepest slumbers. He used that clock when he just had to get up and it woke him up and probably half the street, but surprisingly not the boys, who slept soundly throughout its clanging. He rolled out of bed and fought back the waves of fatigue, which rolled through his head and also the severe aches in his knees and hips. He collected his shorts and vest from the airing cupboard. He left pyjamas there and changed at the top of the stairs and carefully went downstairs, supporting himself on the wooden rail fixed to the wall. Still unsteady on his feet he unlocked the door slipped his feet into his running shoes and staggered down the drive.

Within five minutes of that alarm sounding he was stumbling along the pavement towards the park. Every joint ached initially but gradually, as he warmed up, the discomfort levels dropped, and when he entered the park, his breathing became stronger. Running became easier and after about a mile into the run, began to feel good. He kept the morning run short, no more than 30 minutes, and ran at a pace his body could accommodate comfortably. The more severe, testing session would be later in the day. He returned to the house just under 30 minutes later, sweating profusely, opened the back door to let in Topsy, their tabby cat, which had been waiting on the doorstep. In the kitchen she stopped, looked back and up at him and mewed mournfully for food. He sighed, realised he had no choice and emptied the contents of a strategically-placed tin of her favourite food into her bowl on the floor. Immediately she went to it and started to eat. She must have had a hard night outside.

He listened intently, but there was not a sound. He took off his running shoes, put them on the concrete path outside the kitchen door and crept quietly up to the bathroom for a shower, closed the bathroom door and soon was engulfed by the hot water. Time was pressing however and he towelled and dressed quickly, so as to take Babs her cup of tea in bed, deal with the boys and then get his own breakfast, before the cycle ride to work. They were lucky that morning because Babs was able to drink her tea and wake up properly before the boys woke. Just after 7.30am he wheeled out his bike and cycled to work, apprehensive about his future. It was a fine morning, the autumn sun, already low in a blue sky, showing above the rooftops of the houses on the right side of the road and lighting up the roofs on the left.

On the ride into work he remembered his last discussion with Bernard. Nothing appeared to be good enough for him. He had the slight stoop of many tall men who look down both literally and metaphorically on those around him. He had graduated from Loughborough University with a First in Engineering and had rapidly reached the first rung of management, but then for some reason had stagnated, always being overlooked for higher-level positions. His eagerness to please his superiors was frustrated by his inability to motivate and lead staff and obtain results. He stated regularly that it was his staff's job to provide him with the facts and he would fight their corner with the bosses. But on occasions his firmness deserted him and he sided with the bosses. In meetings with George Fellows, the Commercial Director, to discuss any bid, Bernard made sure to take in with him the engineer who had prepared the bid so as to deflect any criticism onto the engineer rather than himself. George was a smooth-talking salesman, a one-time Naval Weapons Officer, always impeccably dressed in dark single breasted suits, white shirt and blue tie, a stocky man, with large hands and thick fingers in which he constantly turned his favourite burgundy-coloured Parker fountain pen. He had the eternal optimism of the salesman, the order from the customer always about to be received within the next few days. His razor-sharp mind assessed immediately the financial impact of any commercial paperwork put in front of him and also any possible threats to his own future and he was grudging of his time being wasted.

The bid had to be in London by the end of the next month. That portion of the bid being worked on by Peter and his colleagues would have to be into Bernard within the next two weeks for Bernard's own review. Then it would be revised and re-worked by higher levels of management and there would inevitably be late-night working by us and then it would be driven to the Ministry. Too much of the company's future was at stake to trust it to the mails or carrier to take it. Peter had been in Bernard's office the previous afternoon. "We need to go though the final price calculations today, Pete," he had said as they had started. "They have to be with Jimmy by next week so we must put the proposal to bed by tomorrow night." Peter felt Bernard's eyes boring into his skull as he went through the workings. Finally, Bernard reluctantly agreed that the proposal was acceptable. "Right, Pete," he said, "get it typed up for tomorrow and we'll go into George later." Peter took the proposal into the Typing Pool and arranged for it to be typed for the next day.

After work he felt jaded and cycled home slowly, barely conscious of the traffic passing. It had seemed a long day and he was drained, probably because of the early morning run. Still another run could help that and once home he went for nine miles, his second run of the day. After that he felt very tired.

The next day he went into the office, hung his jacket on the coat stand just inside the door of the office, said a cheery "Good Morning," to the world in general. He nodded to Alan, sitting at next desk, but Alan ignored him completely, as though Peter did not exist. Peter looked down at the papers in front of him on his desk. He was the last one in. He glanced at the clock on the wall at the end of the office and saw that the time was 8.25am, still five minutes before the official start time. Everybody was in early. He sat down, puzzled, because this was unusual. He unlocked his desk drawer and withdrew his diary and A4 lined pad and then went to the four-drawer filing cabinet to obtain the files relating to his portion of the contract. He glanced up and saw Bernard looking at him intently through the glass wall of his office. There was no recognition in his gaze and Bernard turned away, to face someone on the other side of his desk, outside Peter's view. This person then moved slightly and his head came into view and Peter recognised Tom Pringle, the Commercial Manager, Bernard's boss. Peter sat down and busied myself with refreshing himself on the details of the bid, all too embedded in his consciousness for them to be forgotten.

After about twenty minutes Peter's phone rang and he picked it up. "Sharpe," he said into the mouthpiece. "Oh, Peter," said the clipped Mancunian accent of Tom

Pringle. "Can you come to my office and bring the Bid contract file with you?" He sounded unusually hesitant and Peter sensed from the tone of his voice that something was different. He had not asked Peter for any file before. Peter got up from his chair, conscious that Bernard looked sideways at him from his office and also sensed that each of the grey heads in the office had tensed up and he knew then that they knew something he didn't. "So was it him for the big heave-ho, the chop, he thought. Well, I've been there before."

He leaned back in his chair, carefully screwed the top onto his fountain pen onto the body, placed the file under his my arm and slowly stood up. He turned to Alan at the and said, "I'm off to Tom Pringle's office. See you later." He sensed, without looking round, that everyone in that office was watching.

He walked slowly out of the office, along the corridor and up the stairs to Tom's office on the second floor, one of a suite of managers' offices. The offices on either side of Tom's were empty. He knocked on the door and almost immediately opened it in response to the "Come in," shouted from within. Tom was standing at the left hand end of his desk, tall, slim, as always elegantly, almost foppishly-dressed, wearing a dark single breasted suit and a dark blue tie over a pale blue shirt, every inch a dynamic professional manager. He was in his mid-thirties, his hair was thinning and he had recently married his long-time girl friend. He had been with the company for about six months and Peter had found him to be correct, meticulous and precise in speech; a company man through and through, but with no sense of humour. He expected his subordinates to understand quickly the main points he wanted to make. He was a decent man without any trace of the nastier, sadistic traits seen in many insecure men who reach higher management levels.

He waved Peter to a chair in front of his desk and then sat down himself. He was nervous, his hand resting on a large, well-filled A4 white envelope on the desk in front of him. Peter knew what it was, but let him make the first move. He cleared his throat. "Well, Peter, I'm sure you must know about the situation in the company. I am very sorry to say we are going to have to let you go."

"Is that the package?" Peter asked, nodding down to the envelope." Tom nodded, "Yes, it is." He handed it across. Peter quickly scanned the top two pages, which contained the salient points relating to the redundancy, and then looked up. He could read the other twelve or so pages constituting the terms and conditions later. He felt that other people, in interviews, would receive a similar letter, which would have been coordinated across the company. He glanced briefly at the terms offered and realised immediately that the company had been generous, having calculated the benefits on four full years, rather than the three years nine months he had actually been there. It represented the best deal he would get. He relaxed and remained expressionless.

There was no point in his becoming emotional or argumentative. There would be no benefit to Peter by his trying to get one back on Tom, who was just doing his job. Peter had learned always to leave a place cleanly, because he might need their goodwill in the future. He had experienced two occasions in which a person leaving a job had spoken his mind savagely to his boss on leaving and had then had to ask for his job back, but, not surprisingly, without success. There was no point in delaying any further, so Peter said, "OK Tom, these things happen. Oh, by the way I don't see much point in my staying here for the rest of the day. Do you?"

He nodded, "Just clear you desk if you will." Peter stood up, shook hands with Tom and went out through the door behind him.

Tom's next visitor soon after Peter was Rob, a friend of Peter's, who worked in another section which also reported to Tom. Tom was almost in tears. Making people redundant can be difficult for the man who has to do it. Peter thought that possibly Tom's behaviour stemmed from his nonchalant acceptance of my redundancy. Who knows?

Peter returned to the office, slightly tensed up, holding the envelope in his hand, determined not to show any emotion. He noticed the curious gazes at him from the men in the office. He went over to Bernard's office, saw that he was looking out through the glass wall at him and Bernard waved him in. He opened the door and sat down on the chair in front of his desk. Bernard smiled sadly. "You must have known about this," Peter said. He nodded, "Yes, I'm sorry Pete, but it's going to happen to a lot of people in the next few weeks. Even I'm not safe."

Peter paused slightly before saying, "I've agreed with Tom that there's no point in my staying here today. I think I might as well go now. That all right with you?"
He nodded. Peter got up, shook his hand over the desk and then went back to his desk. Peter tidied the top of his desk and the desk drawers and put his own possessions into his briefcase. He realised that everyone in the office was looking at him, except Bernard whose head was bent over a document on his desk. Peter said "Goodbye" to every man in the office, shaking hands, just holding back the tears, but managing to keep a stiff upper lip.

"Goodbye, John." "See you around Alan." They appeared stunned, thoughtful and sad. "Oh, I'll arrange a drink somewhere, I'll let you know through Sally." She was Bernard's secretary. Peter then went back to his desk, picked up his briefcase and walked out of the office door. He glanced at the clock on the office wall and was surprised to see it was just 10am Such a lot had happened that morning. He went out into the car park in front of the building and unlocked the padlock, which chained his bicycle to the cycle rack. He wheeled it slowly out through the main gate and made his way home.

He pushed the bike up the drive, wheeled it into the garage and opened the kitchen door. Babs looked up from the washing machine, which she was loading from the blue open weave plastic laundry basket. Her eyes

47

opened wide in surprise. "What are you doing home so early?" she asked. "Have you forgotten something?" He paused, not knowing how to phrase it. "I've been made redundant; just now. Tom Pringle did it, but Bernard knew it all along." He was not as confident, or as much in control now as he had been at work. She came to him, wrapped her arms around and hugged him. "Oh" she said, "What will we do now?" she asked, not really expecting an answer. They hugged each other, almost crying. "Let's have a cuppa," Peter replied. She made the tea, which they took into the front room and he told her about the morning's events.

"Well I can't say I didn't see it coming," he sighed. He then remembered the telephone call and the new interview. "I've got the interview at Henderson's on Friday, that's tomorrow isn't it? I'd better make the most of that one."

"Will you tell them about this redundancy, Pete?" Babs asked.

"Yes, I'll have to I suppose," he replied. "So many people are getting made redundant these days. I'll try to use it as a bonus—say the company is contracting and there have been rumours for some time now. I'll have to look at the paperwork." He got to his feet intending to look at the file he had created relating to the job, but then stopped. "No I need a short run, just to get this lot out of my system."

It took little time for him change into his running gear and soon he was running along the pavements, ignoring the curious looks of the neighbours, curious because it was late morning on a weekday, when most other men were at work. He decided to make this run mean something, no more than half an hour but it had to be hard and as fast as he could make it. After about a mile, he turned right into the park, moving fast now, and his chest was burning. He kept this pressure on himself but gradually felt himself slowing, although his breathing seemed to be just as heavy as earlier. Gradually the bitterness of the dismissal crept back into his sub-consciousness and he slipped into a slower running mode, which he maintained into the drive, which they had shared with Sheila and Harry Jenkins, for 10 years. Sheila was out in the front garden, a pair of pruning shears in her hands, and at her feet was a pile of cuttings from her pruning that day. "No work today, Peter? Got a day's holiday?" she asked suspiciously. Not wishing to antagonise her, although he felt like doing so he just grinned inanely, did not speak and ran past her right to his back door.

Soon afterwards Babs came in with the boys. They immediately took advantage of his unaccustomed presence in the daytime. They changed out of their school clothes and they all went down to the bottom of the garden where the boys immediately climbed their favourite tree, a large alder tree. Some time previously Peter had attached a car tyre to the end of a long rope. The other end of the rope was attached to a high branch and the boys would run down the garden on their return from school, leap onto the tyre and swing over the lower, wet ground underneath them. Looking at them he realised that he needed a job, quickly.

He left the company with one month's pay in lieu of notice and nine weeks' redundancy pay. On the same day the Managing Director, appointed only three months previously, also left the company and his departure so soon after joining may point to the atmosphere within the company.

Their margin for error was small, but he had Bab's support and without her common sense and highly practical approach the next few weeks would have been difficult to survive. It was she who kept him on his toes and who was always ready to prod him along the next avenue towards obtaining a job.

Shortly afterwards he completed a personality profile in an employment agency. His suggested strengths were stated to be:

> A results-oriented self-starter with people understanding. Highly mobile and alert and energetic. Will compete and comply. Is outgoing and gregarious.

His suggested weaknesses were stated to be:

> Can become over-aggressive, blunt and critical. Impatient for results. Could tend to leave if things do not move quickly enough for him.

So, relying on his known strengths and trying to improve his known weaknesses he went out into the big wide world of the jobless.

## 5. Job Search

Domestic matters continued unabated, a new necessity being to increase his stocks of home brewed beer, because now he would be unable to afford many pints at pub prices. Each day had its own priorities which he dealt with rigorously, telephoning to follow up leads, driving to interviews, visiting employment agencies and so on. In this period he applied for many different jobs, some engineering, some completely outside, such as coach driving and cooking at a local pub but he never lost sight of the urgent need to get another permanent job. Like many engineers he had regularly read the Situations Vacant columns in the Daily Telegraph but now he extended the search to the local papers and to employment agencies on the south coast and to the southern fringes of London.

Meanwhile, at every opportunity he kept up the training, taking his running kit with him on every interview, so as to have a run when he was away from home. The marathon itself was now 12 weeks away and marathon performance is closely related to miles run, so he tried to increase the longest distance run in a week, also fitting other runs in whenever he could. In the first week after being made redundant he ran only 23 miles, the longest being 9 miles, the rest much less, restricted by the necessity to complete formalities with the Unemployment Office, contacting agencies, setting up interviews and other matters. "This is not good enough," he muttered to myself after looking at that week's training diary. "I must get out more." Over the next five weeks he managed between three and six runs per week, sometimes just two miles up the road and back, sometimes the luxury of 45 minutes or so, when the heavy sweating and consequential damp running vest lifted his spirits, important because that marathon-goal gave him a necessary focus.

Four weeks after the redundancy Peter ran a five mile road race locally in 28 minutes 10 seconds, not a bad time in retrospect, but as always at the time he was annoyed with himself for not running faster. Then his mileage crept over 30 miles in a week. Two weeks later he ran a one-mile track race, in just outside five minutes and two weeks later still ran a local 10 mile road race in 59 minutes 40 seconds, keeping just inside that 10 mile-in-the-hour barrier. Things were beginning to look up because he managed over 40 miles in one week, including his first run over 10 miles.

When attending interviews his practice was to be smart and clean and his standard dress was a light-grey single-breasted suit, white shirt buttoned down at the wrists and a dark red tie, tied in a small neat knot. He had always considered that knot in the tie to be important because it has always been an eye focus point in person-to-person contact. He wore a white handkerchief in his top pocket, folded to show a small strip of white, parallel to the top of the pocket, continuing habits induced from his service days and social conformity. The top-pocket handkerchief was mainly for show, but every now and again it could serve a useful purpose, such as handing to a lady to wipe herself dry if spilled water or drink went onto her dress, or possibly in exceptional circumstances, with each corner knotted, as emergency protection against strong sun in the absence of a sun hat. He had found that sitting in a car for an hour or more took the smartness out of any suit and also increased the creases around the waist lines so he usually travelled to interviews casually dressed, in an old pair of slacks or jeans and T-shirt and changed into his suit, shirt and tie at the last moment in a motorway service station or in the car if necessary.

In April he went to a session of Open Interviews for engineers, organised by an employment agency in a Leatherhead hotel on behalf of Franconi Systems, a major electronics company. They were recruiting engineers to complete a major contract to design and supply electronics systems. After making good time on the M25, he took exit 10 for Leatherhead, got lost near Epsom racecourse and eventually arrived late at the hotel, 20 minutes later than the scheduled time. He considered this unforgivable and apologised.

He was expected because they had received a copy of his CV from the agency. It was his shortest interview ever. There were two men representing Engineering and one woman from Personnel, a word which in subsequent years was changed to "Human Resources", although in any department he had managed he had always thought that the word "Personnel" described his people better than "Human Resources".

The three were smartly dressed, the men in black suits and with white shirts, the woman in a white blouse and black skirt, and they all appeared to be in their twenties.

The senior of the two men asked him, rather hesitantly, whether he wanted an Engineering post. He nodded, saying that he was not a hands-on engineer, but that he could handle everything else within the engineering environment. The Personnel woman read out a description of the company, and it became embarrassingly evident that they ran out of things to say. Peter kept it going long enough for him to drink his coffee, by bringing out his standard checklist of questions. They agreed to circulate his details and he was handed a brochure of their company products, mainly missile systems and he left, without any high hopes of anything further. Much to his surprise he was invited back four weeks later for interview.

Peter's marathon training continued lightly in these next four weeks, averaging 30 miles per week. On the interview date he left home at 12.30pm, with enough time to visit an estate agent's office in Surrey to obtain brochures on house details before going into the Franconi factory which was situated behind the railway station. The building had a small frontage, which extended back a long way towards the station. It had an old fashioned air about it, high ceilings and wooden block floors.

He changed into his suit in the car and shortly afterwards strode energetically up the steps from the road into a small reception room, towards a smartly-dressed middle-aged lady sitting behind a counter. She wore a fresh white blouse with floral motif, her curly blond hair looking as though she had just stepped out of the hairdresser's salon. He introduced himself, smiling as always to the lady behind the counter. He knew that if you upset these ladies in Reception and they chat informally with the person who interviews you, they can have a damaging effect on your interview progress, especially if he asks, "What did you think of him?" She smiled back. "Please sign the register, Mr. Sharpe."

He signed in, noting the full page of names above his in the column marked "Representing". He wrote "self". There were a small number of company names there, but mostly the word "self", probably of engineers there for interview. He walked over to a low table, picked up a copy of the Franconi newsletter and sat down to read it. He turned the pages slowly, not really concentrating on the contents.

A tall, slim severe-looking lady in a green figure-hugging dress walked briskly out of the corridor on his right, carrying a sheaf of papers in her left hand and a biro pen in her right. She was businesslike, abrupt and unsmiling. "Good afternoon, Mr. Sharpe. I am Jean Windsor, Mr. Hobson's secretary. Can we sort out your travel expenses first before I take you to see him?" They agreed a total, for the train fare (rather than mileage costs for use of the car) and a meal. He signed her receipt and took the money. He followed her along the corridor, and they turned left through double doors into the Production Control Department as stated in capital letters on the left hand wall by the doors. The room extended along a central aisle to another pair of double doors at the far end. On either side of the aisle were two lines of desks, one behind the other, emphasising a familiar air of regimentation. The room was large and the afternoon sun shone weakly through high-level windows, hinged at their lower edge, but open. Lighting was provided by rows of fluorescent lights hanging on long white-painted chains from the ceilings. Each desk had someone sitting at it, mostly slight balding grey-haired men, each bent over studying papers on the desk. Two men were standing talking at a desk on the right. The conversation was subdued. At a glance it appeared to him that no one was aware of his presence, but he sensed that everyone knew he was there and probably why. The department manager, Frank Hobson, occupied the glass-walled office immediately to the left of the entrance door through which Peter had come. He could observe the whole office and also every person coming through that door.

Hobson sat in his chair behind his desk. He wore a white shirt and a striped plain blue tie neatly done up in a compact knot. He appeared to be in his early thirties, had a thin moustache and a strange air of menace. His suit jacket hung on a coat hook in the office. Peter wondered whether the coat hook went with the office and rank of the occupant, as was reputed in the Civil Service. Hobson oozed calm efficiency, and was studying a copy of what Peter saw from the writing was his CV on the desk in front of him. Hobson was seated behind the desk, which was placed with a table in the 'T' arrangement fashionable at the time. Hobson was obviously prepared for him.

They shook hands and he waved Peter to sit, which he did on the right side of the 'T' stem. Peter leaned forward slightly, giving Hobson all his attention. He started by asking about Pipeline, Peter's last-but-one company, in which Peter had been heavily involved in Production. Peter described the Production Control system they had used, the MRP (material requirements planning) system, their use of computers in ordering material and their use of manual override to obtain materials whose requirement was not known until the last moment. Hobson was attentive and pleasant throughout. He showed Peter organisation charts of the Franconi's materials procurement system, his own department having "over one hundred people". The company had a wide range of products, which "utilised every known production technique," he uttered confidently. He then asked about Peter's last company. He was recruiting people who could contribute and communicate. Where would Peter fit in? Did Peter want to go back into Production?

Peter had learned that it in an interview it was essential to appear enthusiastic, even if he was not. He replied, "In all the areas I have worked I've enjoyed Production most because it's the most difficult and yet has boundaries. With Programme Management and Proposals the other dimensions are customers and finance. These present different problems and the boundaries are unknown."

Hobson said, "The job we have available here in Production Control pays £8k. We have requirements and opportunities which change regularly and we have sites all around the country, so there is scope for promotion." Peter was silent for a short time then said, "I have been earning much more than that and in my interviews I have been of the opinion that the right ballpark for me is between £11k and £11.5k. I am really looking for more than what you are offering." He replied," Let me discuss this with our Manufacturing Director. He then added, "At the moment this discussion is purely speculative."

He then took Peter on a tour of the building. Peter was impressed, particularly with the large numbers of printed circuit boards in manufacture. This company had not reached the technology levels he had experienced in his previous companies, but the volumes in manufacture were much greater. The premises were sprawling, but very clean. He liked what he saw but had reservations about differences between salary mentioned, his and theirs and they returned to Hobson's office.

After a pause he asked Peter questions about "Running" as he had mentioned it in his application form and that he was a coach. Hobson had just caught the "Jogging" bug, then sweeping the country. Very softly, but politely Peter said, "I can certainly offer you thoughts on running and how to improve your running performance. "Would you like me to quote you for my services?" He froze momentarily, smiled weakly, but not with his eyes, and shook his head. Peter felt that he had not made a friend there. However, that was not why he had come. Hobson escorted him to the front reception room, where they said their "Goodbye's" and Peter went outside, and blinked in the strong sunlight. He was glad to be outside in fresh air after the slightly soporific air conditioning inside. Some time later he received a standard 'No' letter and wondered if his offer of a quote for coaching services had helped them to send it.

He travelled where necessary for interviews, the longest distance being to Ventura Systems in Elmhurst in Manchester when he flew from Gatwick to Manchester and back in one day. On recovering his travel expenses from a startled Personnel Department man when they sorted out his travel expenses. Peter said, "Air travel is more expensive but there are no hotel bills to pay." He accepted the logic in that and Peter received the expenses without any problems.

## 6. Interviews

After travelling to job interviews and agencies in Surrey and Sussex in mid-July Peter had his first interview with Henderson Systems, the parent company of Henderson Controls. These companies were in the same building. Babs drove him to the main entrance and he walked into a small single storey building, almost hidden behind a low brick wall surmounted by a chain link fence. He went through the doorway marked 'Reception', just as the minute hand on the clock on the wall moved to the two minutes to the hour, the interview time. He went over to the telephonist/switchboard operator behind a counter on the opposite wall and gave his name. She smiled, pressed a key on the console in front of her, leaned forward and said into her microphone, "Mr. Sharpe's here for Ian." Peter was impressed with her use of the first name. After a pause she said, "Take a seat please Mr. Sharpe. Mr. Morris will be down shortly."

Peter sat at a low polished wooden table and turned the pages of a glossy magazine, which described the company products in the process industry. He was surprised and excited to find that he was familiar with the general product lines, because of his employment in that industry some years earlier. He looked up to see a large, florid-faced man, dressed in a grey double-breasted suit across his large stomach, coming across the floor towards him, right hand outstretched. They shook hands. "Please come up Mr. Sharpe," and they went upstairs to his office.

On the wall behind his oval desk was a window, through which Peter could see the leaves of a large tree. The office was quiet, presumably because it was at the back of the building. Morris sat down in his chair behind the desk and reached forward for a pile of A4 sheets of white paper with some typewritten lines at the top of the first. As Peter sat down in the chair on front of the desk facing Morris, he glanced down at the tabletop and saw his name and a copy of the advert he had applied for together with his completed application form.

Morris described the company, relating details fluently without references to notes. Henderson Systems had a turnover of £74 million and was composed of companies of varying sizes, all specialists, in the electrical conductor and connector fields. Their major customers were engaged in supplying electrical equipment, across a number of applications. Henderson Controls, in contrast, was involved in selling instrumentation to the Process Industry, with a product range similar to that of one of Peter's previous employers. Henderson Controls was a small company of six people within the umbrella of the parent company. He stated the requirements for the job advertised. Henderson Controls had a Managing Director, Marketing Manager, Engineering Manager, a technician and two secretaries. "We had a test engineer but we parted company—he couldn't work on his own." He added, "I won't take this further at the moment regarding the test engineer job. We have talked to other people and we have decided to uprate the job."

He then asked about Peter's jobs and Peter was honest. Morris's face became solemn. "These days Mr. Sharpe, it is a good thing to stay where you are." They shook hands and Peter left. A week later he received a letter from Morris saying that a man of his experience was of interest to the company, but the company was very small and no suitable opening was visible. He would place Peter's application on file.

On each of the next two weekends Peter ran 5000 metre races on the track for his club, the first in 17 minutes 15 seconds the second 34 seconds slower. Then, after working all morning to clear the lounge of all furniture so that he could decorate, he travelled to Essex for an afternoon interview with Dextron Avionics, once again receiving a "No" letter ten days later. Then there were open interviews, in Crawley, which resulted in his travelling to Bracknell for a further interview, but once again with the same result.

Four weeks after the first interview with Henderson Systems the advert for a Test Engineer appeared again in the local paper and Peter couldn't resist picking up the phone—nothing ventured, nothing gained. He rang Henderson Systems. "Mr. Morris, I have seen your advert in the local paper." Morris repeated what he had said in his letter, namely that the company had no suitable opening for a man of his experience. Peter then joked, "You know, if you employ me I am captured." It worked, because a few days later, Morris telephoned to arrange an interview with Derek Stanton, their MD, "Just for exploratory purposes."

Four days later he entered the now familiar Henderson Systems reception area and after a few minutes Morris appeared and they walked to the end of the corridor. "Not too stiff then?" he asked, referring to my visit to the osteopath that morning, which Peter had mentioned in the walk from the reception area. Peter muttered, "It's a lot better now, thanks. I've got some movement back into my leg."

They turned right into a large room containing on the right-hand wall, three glass-walled offices, each office having its own rectangular window overlooking the front of the building. In the centre of the large room were three electrical assembly benches arranged in line. Each bench was fitted with a high level shelf with electrical power sockets, test cables hung on hooks and hand tools, together with a soldering iron in its voltage controlled holder.

On the wall opposite to the entrance was another office, this one with solid walls, the office of Derek Stanton. The Henderson Controls MD. He was a tall man, dressed smartly in a dark pinstriped suit. He looked up from the thick file on the desk in front of him and put down his pen. He paused slightly before relaxing again as though irritated by the intrusion. He wore dark thick-framed spectacles and his brown thinning hair tumbled over his forehead. The desktop was completely obscured by papers, some typewritten multi-page documents, which looked like technical specifications. In addition there were blank sheets, with electronic circuits and formulae scrawled on them. Stanton smiled slowly, looked up at Peter, then uncoiled slowly and held out his hand in greeting. His un-blinking eyes were level with Peter's. Morris introduced them.

"Hello. Thanks for coming in." Stanton said, then lowered his body back into his seat, and relaxed as he leaned back and stretched against his chair back. "Coffee?" he asked, as Peter sat down. Peter nodded, thankfully. Stanton looked up at his secretary, but she had anticipated the request and was gathering some cups on a tray. He then described the company operation. The company was small, desperately overloaded, and they were looking for someone to 'help out' with the order entry side-quotations, terms and conditions etc. and also to supervise the testing of products. Peter pricked up his ears at this, because things had obviously changed. They were not talking just a Test Engineer job. Peter concentrated more. Stanton explained that a joint agreement existed between Henderson Controls in the UK and Queensland Systems, an Australian company, to assemble and distribute Queensland's instrumentation products in the UK. They had jointly sold a system incorporating products from both companies and realised they needed someone to straighten out their administration and procedures. He asked about Peter's experience at Pipeline Systems—had he tested microprocessors there and also the modules into which they were assembled on the production lines. Peter's answer was a confident "Yes."

"Can you work in a Sales environment?" he asked. "Yes of course," Peter replied. "I have regularly had to meet customers and discuss technical proposals."

"You have been in a large company handling big proposals. Ours company is very small. How would you handle this?" "The main principles in any proposal are the same. The price quoted should cover all costs and margins, whether it is £20 million or £2000." Peter answered confidently.

Peter described his work in the process industry and then talked over his last job, including the redundancy and mentioned the difficulties the company had been facing. Stanton accepted the fact of the redundancy and was more interested in Peter's work at Pipeline. Peter described his specific testing experience, particularly with components and printed circuit boards, rather than the systems testing, which seemed not to be within this company's requirements "How much direct soldering iron experience have you had recently, although that is not a pre-requisite for this post."
"I've got to be honest, about 10 years ago." Peter replied. "However nothing in what you have described scares me at all. I think I can contribute significantly

to your company. I have always been a shirt sleeve manager."

"I find this conversation encouraging," Derek Stanton said, sinking back into the soft seat and arms of his swivel rocker chair. "We'll be making our minds up in the next two weeks. Oh, on salary we were thinking of the range £9000 to £9,500." He looked at Peter expectantly, "how does that sound to you?" Thoughts raced through his head. "I was thinking of higher than that," he said. "I would be willing to start for £10500." "Would you be willing to come on a month's trial?" he asked and Peter nodded. "Yes, of course."

I want you to talk to Mark Winston, our Engineering Manager. Leave it to me to discuss this with Ian Morris," he said. They shook hands and as Peter walked through the reception area he couldn't help smiling to himself, but tried hard not to show it. He walked out of the front door into the hot late afternoon sun, blinking and almost forgetting where he was. He had been concentrating so hard in there. Four weeks later he received a telephone call from Jenny Davidson, the lady with the "come to bed voice" and they arranged a third interview, this time with Mark Winston, for the following week.

Peter's training was now building up and in early September he surprised himself by running 58 minutes exactly for a 10 mile road race, faster than expected and a rare occasion when he ran faster than his prediction. On the appointed day he entered the Henderson building for the third time. He arrived at the address early so waited a little distance from the main entrance, hidden behind a large oak tree and waited impatiently for five minutes, feeling horribly conspicuous. Once again he walked through the main door just before ten o'clock, the interview time. He waited for over ten minutes for Ian Morris to appear through a door in the right hand wall. "About time too," he thought. Morris started to hum as they walked along the corridor into the same room as before. Peter sensed that things were just not right. Morris appeared tense and said, "We wanted to introduce you to our Mark Winston, our Engineering Manager, but he was called away this morning on an urgent job." Morris took Peter into Derek Stanton's office where Ian Morris left them.

Stanton was standing in the doorway just inside the office. He appeared nervous. "Mark Winston is away on Merseyside—a last minute problem. We wanted you to meet him to discuss your technical knowledge—although I don't consider that absolutely necessary. Since we last talked we appointed a Marketing Manager and he is not coming to us now. We are short-listing, again, and expect to make an appointment within two weeks. If you come in that'll be two new people at the same time. We asked our previous Marketing man to take on some of the Operations but he decided to go elsewhere. We'll get Mark to arrange another meeting with you." Peter then brought out his prepared list of questions and he answered all those relating to the job, as they saw it. He said, "The Personnel type questions will be answered by Ian Morris at your next visit."

It was obvious to Peter that the job scope had shifted away from Engineering towards Operations and this brought the job closer to his background. The salary quoted was now £10500, well below what he had been earning before. But beggars couldn't be choosers. Peter pricked up his my ears when he said, "We understand you have received another offer." Peter realised then that they must have misunderstood something he had said at a previous interview but decided that no harm would be done if was just left as it was. "Yes, it's at a higher salary but it's away from here and I would prefer not to move. My children are at school here."

This gave Peter room to negotiate. His prospects depended on growth of the company. On timescales he said that he would be willing to start during July. When he got home he went out for a run and then got out all the data he could find on microprocessors. He had some reading to do.

## 7. Job Offer

On the next Tuesday morning he received another telephone call from Henderson Controls and agreed to attend for another interview with Mark Winston. This was arranged for the following Thursday at 5.30pm. On that morning he ran five miles. He left home at 5.15pm on his bike, carefully negotiating the rush hour traffic and arrived in reception just before the half hour. The receptionist was behind her desk, talking to a small plump, late-middle-aged grey haired lady, elegant in a grey trouser suit, the shiny toes of expensive-looking grey shoes poking out from below the loose-fitting but smart trousers. In her hand she held an equally expensive-looking grey handbag. She looked as though she was about to leave the building. The receptionist looked up at him and smiled. "Hello, Mr. Sharpe. Mr. Morris will be down shortly." The plump lady looked at Peter, smiled and said, in that memory-dragging sexy, "come-to-bed" voice, "Hello, Mr. Sharpe. We spoke on the phone. I'm Jenny Davidson, Ian Morris's secretary." Peter smiled, hiding his disappointment "Nice to meet you" he replied.

At that moment Ian Morris came down the stairs and across to him. They shook hands and he turned round, waved Peter to accompany him. They repeated the walk down the corridor, into the large room and straight across to the left hand end office of three offices, that of Mark Winston. He was tall and slim, aged about thirty, fair-haired and sunburned with a neat goatee beard. Morris then left. Winston wore a smooth fawn cotton short-sleeved open neck shirt and grey flannel trousers He spoke with a South African accent and Peter could almost feel the dry desert wind on his face.

Winston motioned Peter to a seat in front of his desk. Peter faced the window, through which he could hear the noise of the traffic, now homeward-bound. He reached into his briefcase and pulled out a copy of a technical paper he had written and also specification sheets showing details of devices his team had been testing when he left the USA ten years previously.

Winston appeared impressed. He spoke quietly, but precisely as he described is company products. He showed Peter examples of these products and Peter made appropriate complimentary noises. The instruments were of good quality, compact, functional, well designed, with excellent workmanship. Winston showed Peter the workbenches in the main area of the room. The room was empty, because the working day had ended and this was an ideal time to interview the probable future boss of the people working there. The units sold at between £75 and £230 each, a competitive price for such instrumentation at that time, at the low end of the price spectrum within the industry. Winston explained that the units were manufactured abroad and shipped to the UK for final calibration and assembly into systems.

Henderson Controls intended to enter the UK market with these products and wanted someone, the Operations Manager, to be responsible for all activities from Order Entry through Assembly, Test and Despatch. Mark explained that they needed to institute a paperwork system as soon as possible because they did not have one.

"Your experience has been with a large organisation and your technical expertise is limited." We are very, very small in comparison. How would you handle that?" he asked, staring at Peter intently.

Peter replied, "Big companies by their nature are geared up to large volumes and departments and tend to be inefficient in solving organisational problems. People can hide in them and be carried. I don't want to hide. A small company is compact and flexible, although can have problems with volume orders. But on balance it should be much more efficient." Peter paused and then added, "My kids go to school here, I am unemployed and don't want to move. That's why I can handle the change from large to small."

Peter glanced at the clock on the wall of the office and saw that the time was 7.30pm, so he would have to miss a coaching meeting he had arranged. It had been a long day. Winston opened his door and they walked across the floor to Derek Stanton's office, then to Ian Morris's office, where he took his leave of Peter and then returned to his own office. "I hear that you have got on well with my friends in Henderson Controls, Mr. Sharpe," Mr. Morris said with a smile. We will be making you an offer, with a proving period of one month. I'll ring you in a couple of days."

Peter did not feel it necessary to press for salary details. There was a lot to do in that company and he needed to get his teeth into something difficult. They shook hands and said their goodbyes. Peter walked out through the now-deserted entrance hall, collected his bike from just around the corner and cycled home, slowly, excited and relieved at the prospect of being employed again.

The first job on the next day was decorating. After much deliberation, Babs had decided on the final emulsion for the front bedroom, a light blue shade called "Sky Blue Melt" after 13 or so test colours painted onto hardboard and held up against walls, bed and curtains. But the moment she saw it painted all over she didn't like it. After a further 6 test colours painted on more sheets of hardboard she selected "Ice—White" emulsion. Her decision-making was accelerated by Peter's threat that he was going to apply the emulsion regardless and another coat of Sky Blue Melt was going on unless she really made her mind up. Visitors were expected soon and the room had to dry out.

Peter put an unused 2.5 litre tin of "Sky Blue Melt" emulsion in his haversack, intending to exchange it at the shop where he had bought it. There he could find only two 2.5 litre tins of the Ice White on the shelf and was informed that they did not stock the 5 litre size, which would have been cheaper. Peter had decided to apply three coats of emulsion to make sure that the blue underneath would be adequately hidden, and also apply them with a brush instead of a roller, because of the design of the paper.

He left the shop, but after walking a short distance, decided to buy some new paintbrushes. He returned to the shop, selected the brushes and went again to the long queue at the checkout, putting his haversack containing the tins of emulsion along the smooth tiled floor and slid it along the floor with the side of his foot. He handed over the pack of brushes to the cashier and bent down to pick up the haversack to put them in. He lifted the haversack off the floor but had forgotten to zip up the top. There was a resounding crash as a tin of emulsion slid out onto the floor upside down and the emulsion oozed out onto the floor. Fortunately it was contained in the corner of the wall below the counter and the floor itself.

Silence swept across the checkout queues and Peter grabbed hold of a polythene shopping bag on the counter to contain the paint. A manager appeared at his right elbow. "Spillage?" he asked. Peter nodded and asked for other polythene bags to triple-bag the paint tin that it could be put into the haversack the right way up. "Oh, why don't you get another tin?" asked the manager. Can't." Peter replied, "It's the last one. Don't worry. I'll take it as is." he said. "Do you have any large bags?" The manager nodded and returned shortly afterwards with a few plastic bags in his hands. Peter wrapped polythene around the tin emptied the haversack, then stood the emulsion paint tin and protective polythene upright in it. He then placed the other tin on top, followed by the new brushes and he zipped up the haversack firmly. Finally he stood up, lifted the haversack onto his shoulders, paused and looked at the cashier, then muttered, "It's going to be a long day."

At home, he related the happenings to Babs, who was waiting for him to return so that she could go to work. He made the cup of tea, and then got on with applying emulsion. "This is the last time. It's the last room," He swore under his breath that there would be no more changes. If there were, he was not going to do the painting.

At 9.30 the next morning, he was standing on the steps, applying emulsion to the wall. He intended to finish the second and final coat of emulsion that day. The dressing table, bed and wardrobe were placed in the centre of the room and he had covered them with a large blue plastic sheet. There was a gap of about two feet between the central furniture pile and the walls, just enough to put the steps down in order to paint the walls high up. As he went round the last wall he was getting tired, having been at it for over three hours, but wanting to finish the job at a natural break.

The tin of emulsion was on the floor with the lid off. He placed the Stanley knife on the platform at the top of the steps and moved the steps towards a fresh portion of the wall. The telephone in the hall rang and he jumped at the unexpected noise. The steps rocked gently and he was thankful that they had not fallen over. He heard Babs talking to a friend of hers on the phone. He put his hand onto the top of the steps to pick up the knife, but it was not there. It must have dropped off but he could not see it on the floor, or under or in the folds of the ground sheet covering the furniture. He spied the gaps cut in the floorboards to allow access for the pipes to the radiator. "I know, "he said to himself, "the bloody thing is under the floorboards." Using his screwdriver he lifted the two floorboards, but the Stanley knife was not visible. He was completely stumped. The knife had apparently disappeared into thin air, stupid though it seemed.

He started to clear things away and picked up the tin of emulsion, now one third full. As he lifted it off the floor the tin swung on its plastic handle and there was a low thud. Immediately he knew where the knife was. It had dropped off the ladder straight into the emulsion, which had cushioned the sound of the fall. Using a screwdriver he pulled the knife out of the emulsion. The knife was covered completely with the emulsion, but he cleaned it in a bucket of water and it appeared to function correctly.

The phone rang again. He dropped the roller onto the ground sheet he had spread over that part of the carpet under the ladder. "A good job I put the sheet down," he thought, as he went into the hall, "I wonder who this is." Peter picked up the phone and said, "Good morning, Peter Sharpe."

"Good morning, Peter. Ian Morris here. How are you today? "Oh, all right," he replied, inwardly writhing about the pleasantries. "I'm decorating."

"Ah, you have my sympathies. I am ringing to offer you the position of Operations Manager, terms as agreed yesterday." We'd like you to start on the 18$^{th}$. That's Monday week."

Smiling broadly Peter replied, "That will be fine, Mr. Morris, I accept the offer. Thanks for the phone call." Morris said, "You will receive the letter of appointment in the mail shortly. We look forward to seeing you on the 18th".

Babs looked at him closely as he was speaking and realised before he had finished the conversation that the job had been offered. He put the phone down, looked at her, gathered her up in his arms, kissed her on the lips and spun her round. "They want me to start Monday week," he said, smiling. "How about a cup of tea?" After the tea he went back to the applying emulsion until late afternoon. Then, with the taste and smell of the emulsion in his nostrils, throat and eyes, he needed a run. He changed into shorts and T-shirt and slipped out of the side door, into the rain. "So what," he said to himself, "There's nowt wrong with a drop of rain. I've got another job." He almost raced out of the front door, down the drive and out onto the pavement. He ran hard for the first mile and a half, driven by the adrenalin, fuelled by the excitement after the phone call until natural limitations slowed him to a jog. Then he ambled round the rest of the circuit.

After the euphoria of receiving the job offer he switched his thinking to the marathon, two weeks from the following Saturday. He needed at least one more long run, ideally one long run on a day in which he would run twice, four miles in the morning and 12 to 13 miles later, afternoon or evening.

## 8. Further Interviews

Despite the offer Peter was aware of the possibility that something might go wrong. Once before he had been offered a job, only to have it cancelled before he started, because of a sudden re-organisation which was unknown to the person and division of the company making the offer. So he had to continue with the interviews. Two days later, he drove to Bracknell for an interview with Kineton Developments arranged by a Brighton agency. He left home at 7.30am and drove the 50 miles there, parked in a street near to the Kineton building and changed into his suit. He went in through the tall double glass doors into a very smart entrance hall, just before the interview time of 9.45am. He moved cautiously across the polished tiled floor to the lady at the reception desk, behind which a lady was talking into a telephone. She stopped her conversation and asked to him to sign in and this he did. He then smiled and walked across towards a low and started to read the obligatory company magazine.

Some time later he heard a slow measured sound of footsteps and saw a tall man dressed in a dark brown worsted suit, coming into view on an open-plan spiral staircase opposite. He walked on the outside of each step, his left hand sliding down the shiny brass rail as though to prevent himself from falling forwards. He eased himself down the remaining flight of six steps and sidled over to Peter, right hand outstretched. "Mr. Sharpe," he said, smiling, "Thanks for coming along. Please come up." He was short, late 30's, with curly ginger hair.

They went upstairs and he talked. "My name's George Fowler. I'm Technical Director here. My secretary's off somewhere, so I came down myself to collect you." They walked up the stairs, turned left down a corridor into large empty plan office containing some desks and drawing boards. Beyond them was an open space, "Room for expansion, Mr. Sharpe. We can get another ten desks there if we need them," he said, puffing himself up. They went into his office, which was on the extreme right hand end of a row of empty offices, which stretched across the far end of the main office. "This was used by TPI (a well-known electronics media company) for R&D before we bought it from them," he said, as though explanation were needed.

Fowler indicated with his hand a brown leather-upholstered chair in front of a large rectangular wooden desk, an unspoken invitation for Peter to sit down. Fowler walked round the desk and eased himself into the large black leather swivel rocker chair, letting out an almost audible sigh of relief. He looked up at Peter. "Please sit down." When seated in the chair he became part of it and seemed to change personality. "It looks as though this is going to be very confrontational," Peter said to himself.

Peter sat in the chair indicated, taking time to ensure that he was comfortable. Fowler talked about his workload for what seemed a long time and moaned about his lot. Then he described the company and the type of person they were seeking to recruit. Kineton were part of HB Holdings whose chairman was planning 100% annual growth. They needed someone—a Project Co-ordinator person—to monitor all jobs, starting with finding out the status of each job. The successful applicant would be expected to help on some quotes and do some production control. He had attended to these functions himself, but it was now necessary to recruit someone else. The major project control tool in place was PERT (Project Evaluation and Review Technique) a well-known project control system, introduced, like so many such systems, from the USA.

Looking at him Peter felt that he would not let much authority be delegated. Fowler stated that the salary of

£10.5k was within his budget for the right man. "I've had a number of letters from good candidates. He then read to Peter a letter from an applicant, saying at the end, "He's a good man." Peter saw no need to comment. In the end Fowler asked about Peter's expenses and he dictated over the phone the wording for a petty cash voucher to his secretary. Peter quoted 50 miles each way and collected the money on the way out.

He felt that he could do the job and make a significant contribution to that company but suspected that Fowler did not know what he wanted and Peter was suspicious of his management abilities. Peter was not sorry to receive a 'No' letter ten days later. It was fortunate that he had received an offer from Henderson Controls.

## **9. The Marathon**

That year Peter's training had gone as well as he could have hoped, considering the redundancy and in the 16 weeks before the marathon week he averaged just over 41 miles per week, which for him was a lot. This was achieved by running about five and a half miles a day on most days, with long runs, usually on Sunday mornings, and faster sessions on track or road. On the day of the race he was aged 39.

The race started at 2pm and they left home at 9.30am, Peter and three others packed into Dave's Ford Consul for the two-hour drive to Harlow. As usual in these race day journeys conversation was about Athletics and specifically, running, all family and job cares being pushed firmly into the background. They discussed their own training, times achieved and also the times they hoped for in this race, the likely winner and recent results of races around the country. The drive was smooth, with a toilet stop at a service station and they arrived at the stadium just before midday. There was adequate time to prepare for the race.

The race started on the running track and followed a three-lap course along cycle paths and quiet roads and the race finished on a road near to the stadium. It was overcast, the temperature was sixty degrees Fahrenheit, and it was not likely to warm up. Conditions were ideal and he would not wear a cap.

They went over to register and collected their numbers and pins from the officials seated at trestle tables in an open-fronted tent. On the tables were piles of numbers, a pile of programmes and a box of safety pins for attaching the numbers to the fronts of the vests. They joined the short line of runners who were waiting to register. Seated at the table was a grey-haired man wearing a British Amateur Athletics Board (B.A.A.B) badge on his dark blue blazer pocket and a white shirt and B.A.A.B. tie. In front of him was a race programme, which he used to tick off the names of the runners as they reported to him and if they had paid the entry fee. They gave their names, collected their numbers and pins and walked quietly away from the table. All they had to do then was to pin their numbers onto their vests and be on the start line. After looking at the sky and wind speed and direction, Peter decided that he would wear a T-shirt under his club vest, and shorts.

As the start time approached, the runners milled about, some warming up seriously, some walking slowly, some joking nervously. Others were silent and contemplative. Some talked earnestly with other athletes. The group of 200 or so runners moved en-masse along the finishing straight, closer to the start. Peter moved towards the back of the field, knowing what would happen in the front ranks when the gun went. Then, with everybody quiet, the referee shouted course directions to the assembled and nervous runners, with no one listening and then handed over to the starter. There was a pause, a silence and then a sharp 'Bang'.

There was a relieved and audible sigh of relief from the runners, some nervous giggles and then the race was on. Peter had his usual target of 40 minutes per 10k, which if continued throughout the race, would result in a time of 2 hours 48 minutes. This would be a significant improvement on his previous best of 2 hours 59 minutes 30 seconds, set three years previously. In each of his last two marathons he had used the same starting pace, but in each case had slowed dramatically in the latter stages of the race. He started cautiously and the first 10k marker was passed in 41m 03s and he had not really got into his stride. Gradually tensions dropped away and at the 20k marker his watch showed 1h 20m 57s, the second 10k having taken 39 minutes 54 seconds. He was excited because he was so comfortable and right on his schedule for a good time. He was running with big Richard Davis, a sergeant in the paras, who, with a number of his colleagues, later served in the Falklands. Richard was tall, with thick curly hair, a strong Yorkshire accent, who had always beaten Peter. He spoke precisely, was economical with language and he and Peter had always got on well.

After the 20k marker, when Richard and Peter had been running shoulder-to-shoulder, helping each other along by chatting, until Richard was there no longer and the chatting stopped. Peter expected Richard to appear at his shoulder at any moment and pushed on, the intense aches rising through his body, from his feet upwards. He was running easily, comfortably and the 30k check point was reached in 2h 2minutes 32s, the last 10k taking 41 minutes 35 seconds. "I'm going to break 2 hours 50," he said to himself confidently but foolishly, because of the inevitable slowing down over the last part of a marathon. Reality set in and he realised that he was not going to do the hoped-for 2h 48m.

Over the last ten miles, as the pain gradually spread upwards from his feet through his body to his head he just kept going, passing the 40 kilometre point in 2h 43m 22s, the last 10k having taken 40 minutes 50 seconds. Now he was in survival mode and everything was hurting. He had to 'keep going and was on his own, despite having other runners close by, in front and behind, but each totally confined within his own private painful battle. The stadium came into view and he turned the corner to see the finish through a curtain of sweat over his eyeballs. In that 300 or so metres to the finish, he leaned forward until the finish line passed under his feet and he could stop. He pushed the 'stop' button on his watch with relief as he crossed the finish line. In fear and desperation he tried to focus his eyes onto the watch face and did not at first believe the 2˙

hours 52 minutes 59 seconds shown there. This was a personal best by over six minutes and he finished 88th out of 140 finishers. He was annoyed with himself because he had been on for a much faster time early on in the race. He had actually speeded up between 30 and 40 kilometres, but had then slowed, inevitably. But you can never argue with a personal best (pb).

He stood upright, looking along the line of runners, many looking skywards, most running a wobbly line and saw Richard coming up the finishing straight. Peter had been driven by fear over the last few miles, fear that Richard would catch him. Then Richard crossed the line, looking grey and gaunt and they both staggered painfully to the trestle table on which orange and other drinks had been placed. Peter picked up a white plastic cup, drank the orange squash and then another. Then they both met up with John and Dave to discuss the race, times and the performances of other runners. "Where were you Richard?" Peter muttered through parched lips, "I was expecting you from 30km on."

"Oh, you just went away. I couldn't stay with you, Pete," he replied. They then made their painful way from the track to the changing rooms, commiserating with each other. They met up with the others for the journey home and as usual talked about nothing but the race itself.

## 10. Back to reality

It was after seven pm by the time Peter got home. He and Babs made their way into the kitchen and had a light meal, which was normal practice after a race. "I had a good one today, Babsie, I took six minutes off my pb." She smiled, "Oh that's good." Then the subject was changed and they discussed house and family matters as normal in the evenings.

Peter's mind moved forward to the next week and to starting his new job in just over a week's time. The next morning he woke feeling as though every bone and joint in his body was held in a vice, and hurting. He was not surprised, having experienced it previously after a marathon and knew that the remedy was a short run, painful though it would be. He dressed in tracksuit bottoms, two long-sleeved tops and ran slowly out of the drive and went round a three-mile circuit towards the town centre, keeping on the grass as much as he could. He knew that he was running slowly and would take 35 minutes to run the three miles, rather than the normal 18 minutes. After the run he had a hot bath, as hot as he could bear it. The next day he repeated this run and found that most of his joints and muscles were feeling easier, although he was not running any faster. On the next two days he did not run at all.

His main objective now was for the next week to pass and for him to get back into the security of a regular job and of course a regular income. But in that week he was able to run on five days out of the seven. His enforced spell of inactivity was due to end so he applied myself to getting some decorating out of the way and also looking after the boys. A week with a young family soon goes.

## 11. Back to Work

That first day came at last and he was first up in the house well before 6am (his normal time was 6.45am). He was unusually meticulous in washing and shaving and dressed initially in jeans and T-shirt. After breakfast he changed into the newer of his two suits. Then, watching the minute hand on the clock on the mantelpiece of the front room, he put his briefcase into the haversack, kissed Babs. "Good luck," Babs said. He paused, got on his bike, lifted his left hand from the handlebars in quiet salute and set off slowly towards the industrial estate, to his workplace sanctuary.

Everybody welcomed him, sensing, as with every new employee, that he would be nervous. He went first to Ian Morris who detailed the organisation and procedures and was then taken to Derek Stanton and then Mark Winston. The Marketing Manager's office was empty, the new man expected within two weeks. On the way through the main office he was introduced to Frank, his technician whom he had noticed sitting at one of the benches, looking at him cautiously. Peter was to be his new boss. Frank was tall, grey haired, in his late fifties, with large brown-framed spectacles. He wore a green polo neck sweater and grey flannel trousers. They both smiled as they said, "Hello," mechanically.

Then Morris introduced Peter to two women were sitting at desks situated just outside Derek Stanton's office. They were the two secretaries. He had already met Jean, Stanton's secretary. She had blond hair brushed straight down both sides of her head, smartly and soberly dressed in a charcoal-grey trouser suit. At the other desk sat a tall brunette, in her late twenties, wearing a light blue dress, with a light blue kerchief around her neck. She was Margaret, who would be Peter's secretary and she would handle all the production correspondence, report typing and documentation.

Apart from the absent Marketing Manager the whole company labour force of six people was in that room. This was a strange sensation for Peter after the large departments he had worked in until then, with the management staffs very remote, living and working in their ivory towers and mahogany-row environments. This was different and he relished the difference.

After being made redundant in May, within the first two weeks he had contacted seven agencies and three companies. It took over five months before he obtained his next job and in that time he made out 69 job applications, was asked to attend 17 interviews and received one job offer. In the end the family stayed in their house, the boys stayed in their local school and Peter was able to continue training for the marathon. In this new environment he wanted to work, to forget the agonies and despair of doing the rounds of employment agencies and company reception areas. He was tired of interviews with hard-pressed managers, many not knowing what they were looking for in a new employee. Most wanted someone who could eliminate their problem areas, without being a threat to them personally and at a low enough salary they could afford.

Peter was employed again and also preparing for his next race. One week after the marathon, towards the end of October the cross country season started with cross country relays and he ran his best time for years on a three mile leg in a local cross country relay. The next week he set his fastest time over a local five mile cross country race. The marathon preparation had improved him all round. The world and running go on and on.

END

# CHAPTER 3

# STOLEN HATS—AN INTRODUCTION
# TO ATHLETICS

I started to run while I was in the Royal Air Force (R.A.F.) in Germany in 1954 when I was 19, just to get off the station at weekends and sometimes in the middle of the week. On returning to Civvy Street in the autumn of 1955 at the age of 21 I did not know what I wanted to do, and after a few months working as a labourer on building sites I joined the Metropolitan Police in February 1956. After 3 months training in Peel House, just off Vauxhall Bridge Road, I served at Paddington Green Police Station. Paddington is probably best known because of its main line railway station, but also because of the Victorian song "Pretty Little Polly Perkins of Paddington Green" and the more recent exploits of Paddington Bear, in children's books. The area policed by this station included the Bayswater Road along the north side of Hyde Park, from Marble Arch to Queensway in Bayswater and north along both sides of Edgware Road. This whole area contained every elements of society, every aspect of crime and human behaviour. It was a comprehensive introduction to big city policing and I consider myself fortunate to have had the experience. However this experience probably accounts for my jaundiced and cynical view of human behaviour.

On the last day of August that year in I was on Late Turn (2 to 10pm) and in the middle afternoon was the sole occupant of the police canteen. In came the Patrolling Officer, his face flushed and concerned. "What are you on, lad?" he asked.

"14 and 15 beats Sarge," I replied and continued that I had booked in for an official tea break.

"Come with me," he said and we went outside to his car. He drove down to the Lancaster Court Hotel, just north of Hyde Park. On the way he explained that some Russians were at the hotel and there had been some incident. He did not know the details. I had to control the traffic outside the front steps of the hotel and "Keep the Peace."

We drove the short distance to Lancaster Gate and he stopped the car by the kerb outside the front door of the hotel. It was just a peaceful sleepy, sunny afternoon. It appeared that two days previously the Russian (and Olympic) women's discus champion, Nina Ponomoreva, had been arrested and charged with stealing five hats from C & A's in London's Oxford Street. She had been bailed into the custody of an Embassy official to appear at Bow Street Magistrate's court the next day. She had not appeared in court and a warrant had been issued for her arrest.

The Russians reacted bitterly to this "dirty provocation" against one of their athletes and called off the Athletics match scheduled to be held on that Friday night, 31st August and Saturday 1st September at the White City Stadium. The athletes had returned mournfully to the Lancaster Gate Hotel while the diplomats tried to sort out the mess. It may be that the Russian officials thought that the British government would overturn the judicial process as they probably could in their own country. To help the reader to understand what all the fuss was about it must be remembered that then the Cold War was at its height and spy-mania was a permanent feature.

I stationed myself outside the front of the hotel, keeping a few cars' length space clear directly in front of the main entrance, mindful of my sergeant's instructions. From time to time cars pulled up into the space, dropped off passengers who went into the hotel and then the car moved off. After about 30 minutes a large black car with one occupant drew up and parked right in the middle of the open space. The driver, a tall, lean, balding, middle-aged man, smartly dressed in a dark suit and tie, got out and walked round his car and started across the pavement to go up the steps into the hotel.

"Move your car, sir." I said, walking up to him.

"But I am Jack Crump."

"Move it," I said firmly.

He turned, walked around the car, looked despairingly at me, opened the car door and drove off. I had no idea who he was. He was of course the secretary to the British Amateur Athletic Board (B.A.A.B.) and was deeply immersed in the political and complex negotiations involved with trying to salvage the Athletics match scheduled to take place at the White City that night and the next day. That match did not take place. The Russian team went home the following Monday and Ponomoreva later appeared briefly in court, was fined and shortly afterwards she followed the rest back to Russia.

However, that day, well before they returned home, I was able to do my little bit to further the cause of Anglo-Soviet Athletics relations. As I kept the traffic and growing crowds of the press and curious onlookers under good-humoured control, I noticed people at the windows of the hotel looking down at me, all with mournful expressions. I mentioned this to the driver of one of the coaches being used to transport the Russians around. His coach was parked by the kerb, outside the open gap, which I controlled. The other coaches, hired from a British company, were parked up the road, just out of my sight.

"Why are they so miserable?" I asked. "Are they always like this?"

"No" he replied," They think you are here to spy on them."

I was astounded.

"That's crazy," I replied, "How can I spy on them with this uniform and this helmet?" pointing up to my black dome-shaped British bobby's helmet.

"You go and tell them that I am here to protect them, to keep the traffic under control."

He went into the hotel and the reaction was miraculous and almost instantaneous. The frowns changed to smiles and the Russians came out for walks. Most smiled at me and I had my photograph taken between their male and female shot putters. As I was just above the lower height limit for the Metropolitan Police (5′ 8″) and they were both at least 6′ 6″ the top of my helmet was just at the level of their eyebrows. I have not seen that photograph but would like to.

Later that day I had the pleasure of shaking the hand of Vladimir Kuts on his return from a training run in Hyde Park. My main recollection of him was of a stocky, wiry man, just taller than me, with piercing blue eyes in a bronzed face and the long blond hair swept back behind his head. In Moscow eleven days later he broke the world record for 10,000 metres. I tried to chat up Nina Otalenko, the petite, dark-haired Russian 800 metre champion. I knew no Russian, she knew no English, but she had a delightful smile.

I must have done something right that day because later, in mid-afternoon, I was invited into the hotel by one of the hotel staff, and directed into a small room where I sat down at a table on which was a tray piled high with sandwiches and a large jug of coffee. Maybe Jack Crump did not have any hard feelings towards me because he gave me an official's ticket, which allowed me into the White City Stadium for any Athletics match. I mislaid it and found it some months later and used it at the White City on the evening of 19 July 1957 for my first Athletics meeting and saw Derek Ibbotson run 3m 57.2s for the mile and break the world record. Going into that race the world record was 3 minutes 57.9 seconds, set by the Australian, John Landy and even now, over fifty years later, I can still hear the announcement of the result. Nowadays the announcer will say, "The result of the race, in a <u>new</u> world record, is . . . ." In 1957 at the White City the practice was for the announcer to give just the time. He announced the words, "three minutes fifty seven point two . . ." and the remainder of the announcement was lost in the uproar of the 70,000 or so people in the stadium. A few months later I started running cross-country for the Metropolitan Police.

As a sequel to the above happenings I met Jack Crump some years later in the bar of the train taking athletes from Euston to the North of England for the National Cross Country Championships and related the story. He grimaced at the recollection of that hectic day but relaxed as he mentioned the benefits to British Athletics from that incident. It took the Russians a long time to obtain further Athletics matches with Great Britain and after they had agreed to improved terms and conditions.

In 1959 I left the Police, started a job as a Laboratory Technician at Reading University and joined Reading AC and started my lifelong involvement as a runner with a number of Athletics Clubs, which has been sustained to this day.

END

# CHAPTER 4

## ATHLETICS FOLKLORE

Athletics, like most human activities, has its own folklore, its own stories, mostly part-remembered, often exaggerated in the telling and the re-telling. Reputations can be made or destroyed, forever. It is said that "The Road To Hell Is Paved With Good Intentions." So it can be with the folklore stories. The best way to illustrate this is to relate a story as it actually happened. We go back to June 1974 when I entered the famous Polytechnic marathon, which started in Windsor Castle and ended on the running track in Windsor. I was hoping for a good time (for me that is) but my training had been hit and miss and I had not run many miles in the weeks before the race. Like many runners, I was willing to experiment with any idea, which held any promise of a better time.

At the time I worked in Redhill and every day went to work in a car driven by Arthur, a work colleague, who lived at the end of my street. In his younger days Arthur had been a serious competitive cyclist, a sprinter. We were about the same age and every day we discussed or argued about our own sports and the world in general.

Often we talked about the Tour de France, the World's most prestigious cycling race. We often talked about the rapport between endurance cyclists and runners and one day we were discussing methods used by cyclists to improve their performances, particularly in the mountain sections and when it was very hot. Arthur told me that one trick the riders used in the Pyrenees in summer to keep their heads cool was to wear a lettuce leaf on their heads, kept in place by the caps which they all wore. With the marathon coming up I decided to try this and on the day of the race took with me lettuce leaves, moistened under the cold water tap in the kitchen.

In the hope of achieving a faster time and convinced or conned by articles appearing in the Athletics magazines, I decided to use drinks and decided on orange squash diluted with water for fluid replenishment during the race. This was my first attempt with taking drinks in the marathon, It was a very hot day and I remember well the stables at Windsor Castle where we changed for the race. The cobbled floor of the stables was covered with peat and wooden trestles tables and wooden forms were provided for use by the competitors for changing. The atmosphere was hot and oppressive, although not obviously with rich horse manure, which surroundings hinted at. Conversation among the athletes was subdued and I changed into my shorts and vest, to which I had pinned my race number with the inevitable four safety pins, one for each corner. Next to me was a group of three Japanese runners, one of whom was the eventual winner of this race. I laced up my shoes and then pulled out of my sports bag my white baseball cap, the sort worn by most runners that day, and also my dampened lettuce leaf in its polythene bag. Just before we went outside I withdrew the lettuce leaf and placed it into my cap, before putting put the cap onto my head. The Japanese trio watched the process with startled concern. Then we were called out to the start of the race, just outside the door.

The race started at the beginning of the Long Walk with the castle behind us. The starter fired his gun and we were off. I started well enough, the skin on my arms and under my vest sensing the heat. I took my first drink at the first feeding station but before the five-mile point I felt heavy, my mouth felt sticky and sweet and I realised that something was wrong. "Maybe I didn't dilute the orange squash enough", I thought. Things got worse and I slowed gradually and round about eleven miles I stopped and called it a day. It was the first time that I had ever dropped out of a race and I was bitterly disappointed. In retrospect my training in the 12 weeks before the race had been about 35 miles a week and it was just not enough, because to run a marathon seriously you need more miles.

We went home, commiserated with each other and I tried to drive the thought of not finishing out of my mind, but couldn't. At the time I was the editor of a club newsletter, which I printed on a second-hand Roneo-Vickers tabletop duplicator. This machine used a lot of ink and took hours to print the copies required. Each month my wife and I would set up the duplicator on our dining room table, which experience had told us to protect well with newspapers and cloths because of the excess amounts of ink which somehow did not stay on the pages of the newsletter. On memory the newsletter was of two A4 pages, double sided. We lost a lot of page 1 when we printed page 2 on the back and the same with pages 3 and 4. I handed the newsletters to club members on training nights in the cloakroom of a local school which the club used on training nights, and I derived much satisfaction from the intensity with which the athletes stopped what they were doing when I handed them their newsletters. Changing stopped while they sat down and read the latest news.

In the first issue in the newsletter after the marathon I wrote about my lettuce leaf episode. Nothing was said then, but afterwards, occasionally someone would mutter about a "lettuce leaf", then "cabbage leaf", accompanied by a furtive look in my direction and a smile. It was all good fun.

Over thirteen years later, in November 1987, I left Crawley to start a job in Barrow-in-Furness in Cumbria and shortly afterwards, on a visit down south, I went to Parliament Hill in London to watch the National Cross Country Championships and enjoyed it enormously, being able to shout at runners from two clubs in the race, Crawley and Barrow. After the race I was running round the course and saw two Crawley vests worn by runners whom I did not recognise. I jogged up to them and introduced myself, saying, "Oh, hello my name is Barry Worrall . . . ." I was going to add, "I was a member of Crawley AC," but was not given the chance. "One of them interrupted me and said "Was it true about the cabbage leaf . . . ?"

Much later, in 2005 my wife and I realised that our large family house in Cumbria, with its view of Coniston Old Man fifteen miles away, was too big for us and more importantly that running costs and maintenance efforts were moving out of reach. We decided to sell up and buy a smaller property and move back down south so as to be near our grandchildren. Four years later, in April 2010, I went to Sutton Park near Birmingham, the regular venue of the National 12 Man Road Relay Championships. There I was able to support the team from Barrow in their first visit to this event since 1996, when I been there with them. Some details of that day may be seen in Chapter 9, Running, Sex and Beer. While walking round trying to find the Barrow team I spied a face, now middle-aged and much fuller than I remembered some many years previously. I had last seen him when he had been in his very early twenties. I went up to him, stood right in front of him and said, "Hello Jeff." He paused, looked puzzled. "I bet you don't know who I am," I said, grinning.

"He smiled, slowly, puzzled, "I recognise the face," he said, apologetically.

"Barry Worrall." I said, grinning," How are you?"

He looked up at my baseball cap, lifted his hand and gently lifted the cap off my head, "I was looking for the lettuce leaf," he replied and we both burst out laughing. That was the start of an enjoyable conversation.

After my disastrous run and early exit from that particular Poly marathon, malicious rumours circulated among our runners and these must now be denied categorically, as follows:

1. It was not true that I dropped out because of greenfly.
2. I was going to try savoy cabbage or Brussels sprouts next time.

END

# CHAPTER 5

# THE 1970 BOSTON MARATHON—MY FIRST

This account, written for friends in England, was an attempt to describe my thoughts, impressions and fears during the period in which I trained for the Boston Marathon and the race itself. For the benefit of my friends in England I provided a translation in brackets immediately following any word which reflected a particularly American-English usage.

In the minds of the public the two running races which stand out as being most worthy of note and excitement are the mile and the marathon. The former is over in less than four minutes on a cinder or synthetic running track while the latter takes more than two hours on roads. In eleven years of competitive running at all distances from 100 yards to 12 miles for various clubs in England, Canada and the United States I often thought that there was a gap in my Athletics education, caused by my never having run a marathon.

## THE 1970 BOSTON MARATHON—MY FIRST

I suppose that it was in the five years up to 1970 that I thought many times of running a marathon but never actually did it. So at the ripe old age of thirty-five and going to live and work in the Boston area, the possibility of running this world-renowned and long-lived race moved to the forefront of my thoughts. But before I could run it, I had to move down there from Montreal in Canada and find a place to live. Running had to take second place to moving in.

With my wife Val and young family, children Michael (aged two) and David (fifteen months) and all our furniture I left Montreal on 20 September 1969 to move to Massachusetts in the USA and it was not until the end of October that I contacted the secretary of Spartan A.C., in the town of Brockton, with a view to carrying on running. Brockton's main claim to sporting fame is that it was the birthplace of Rocky Marciano, the one-time Heavyweight Champion of the World. At that time running the marathon was for me a dream because to run three miles was an effort. I had to start the long slow process of building up strength. First came a three mile run, then five miles and then as a real adventure a laborious seven miles one Sunday. Then ten miles became my longest run. Two cross country races, one in November (3.5 miles) and one in December (6 miles) demonstrated improvement, but, how slow I was running. I suppose that the few months during which I had not run at all because of changing jobs and moving in had not really impaired my basic strength, built up over years of involvement in this fascinating and demanding sport, but had merely made me run slower.

Christmas came with no great running achievements behind me. I had settled in at work and attended to all those details associated with changing not only job, but country as well. However a plan of campaign was forming in my mind as to how to handle the Boston Marathon, which was scheduled for mid-April. It would be the 74th running of the race. In New England, January and February were reputed to be cold although the weather was notoriously unpredictable. But I felt confident that after surviving nearly three Canadian winters in Montreal nothing the New England climate could offer would worry me. It turned out that I was right. After Christmas 1969 my training started in earnest. The target of forty miles per week was the immediate target, sometimes met, sometimes not. Runs of seven miles became regular, extending to ten or twelve miles on a Sunday run. Soon my knowledge of local geography became extensive and a surprised colleague at work would approach me and would say, "Was that you I saw running in the snow last night"? When running at low temperatures (say, from zero to 32 degrees Fahrenheit, (minus eighteen to zero degrees Centigrade) extreme care must be taken to protect the body against the cold and strong winds. I found it adequate to wear a bri-nylon lightweight ski-jacket over several shirts, vests, etc. A woollen hat could be pulled down pulled down over the ears when needed and a hood on a ski jacket served as a first protective layer for the head in very cold weather. Sweatsuit (tracksuit) bottoms and heavy training trainers covered the legs and feet and woollen or cotton gloves completed the sartorial ensemble.

With the advent of dark evenings and the occasional snowstorm, along with temperatures well below freezing I took to wearing a bright orange-coloured reflecting vest over my ski jacket. This provided an early warning to approaching drivers that I was on the road. It was interesting to note that on a car some distance away on a dark country road the main beam would flick up to pick me out. It was amusing and provided me with food for thought when the headlights of a car approaching me on a long road would suddenly leap out into the centre (center) of the of the road, as if hit by a giant hammer. The driver had suddenly seen me.

On country roads it was my practice to run on the left side of the road, facing oncoming traffic. Although I am shortsighted and must wear spectacles while driving a car, I did not then wear them while running. Despite this, I made a point of observing carefully the path of every approaching car. I would observe the change in size of the gap between the side of the car and the edge of the road and this could be difficult on country roads with no kerbs, especially after a snowfall. This practice stood me in good stead one evening when I was running along a straight road and approaching a car which was parked facing me on the other side of the road about 50 yards away. Fifty yards past the car the road turned to the left. It was a cold night, the temperature about 20 degrees Fahrenheit (12 degrees of frost) and I was running into a headwind of about 10 miles per hour. The sky was cloudless and the stars shone intensely as if each intended to light up the sky on its own.

Across the open fields to my left I could see the reflections of the stars and trees in the smooth mirror-like surface of the field, now encased in its ice cover. I was running hard, protected from the wind by my ski jacket, with the normally folded hood erected over my woollen hat. I was aware of my heavy breathing, and then the sound of a high-revving car engine. The car sounded fast and the headlights appeared in the sky around the bend in front of me and then the headlights shone into my eyes as the car sped straight toward me. Despite the headlights I still managed to focus on the distance between the near side of the car and the edge the road and it was not enough. The car was fast as it went into the bend and I thought he would hit with the parked car. However the driver corrected and with a noiseless jerk the headlights swung towards the parked car, out and then towards me. The car came straight for me but my instincts were quicker. Without my thinking my left leg landed in the ditch at the side of the road and I felt the freezing water on my leg just as the car passed me. I doubt if the driver saw me.

Most of my running was on country roads, past many houses and in contrast to England there are no or very few fences or wall. Between the road and the houses is grass, driveways (drives) and occasional trees. The house foundations are made of concrete and rest of the superstructures are made of wood and are all detached. Most of the houses are single-storey, having a similar floor area to an English three bedroomed detached bungalow. However the majority have the very comfortable addition of a basement of the same floor area, so effectively doubling the floor area. Further north in Canada basements are essential to take the foundations below the frost line. The houses are spread out at all angles to the road and have lot sizes, which are much bigger than those in England. There appears to be no shortage of land.

As I ran down a country road, or semi-country road, with houses on each side I noticed the mailboxes by the side of the road, at the end of each drive. "Please Mr. Mailman, please," they seemed to say. The U.S. mailbox is an aluminum (aluminium) box 19 inches long, 6 inches wide and 9 inches high. Sometimes they were painted, sometimes not. The name of the owner was painted on the side. The ends had flat bottoms and the sides had a semi-circular top. At the front of the mailbox next to the road was a door, hinged at the bottom, shaped to just seal the end when closed. The mailbox was usually mounted on a wooden stake about four feet off the ground. This sensible arrangement enabled the mailman (postman) to deliver the mail (post) without getting out of his car. On some roads, even where houses were on both sides all mailboxes were on one side—so allowing the mailman to pass down that road on one side only. The American flag was much in evidence on houses, flagpoles, in gardens, on gravestones in the churchyards.

## TRAINING

January saw 167 miles run, in varying conditions. This month included a four-day business trip to San Francisco during which I ran twice in warm rain rather than the snow of New England. Late January saw the removal of four of my top teeth (including a back tooth with extremely large roots). In this period in the USA I had frequent dental treatment and I would not run on the day of the extraction, but would run the day after. However the extraction of the back tooth caused a mild reaction, which interfered with training for a few days. In these visits to the dentist, my secretary could not understand why I would have a tooth extracted in the morning and go straight back into work. She fully expected me to take the rest of the day off at least, like other people in the company. I did just what I normally did, although I knew of many people later in my career who would have taken whatever time off that they could.

The 28 days of February contributed 164 miles, the maximum training distance being 14 miles. My longest ever race up to then, (20 miles) took place that month. It started in Hopkinton, the starting point of the Boston Marathon itself and covered the first 17 miles of the marathon course before turning off and finishing in a suburb of Boston. My time was 2 hours 19 minutes and the last hour was just misery. This particular race indicated to me the limitations of the training I had been doing. Tiredness and desperation were my constant companions in the late portions of the race and I had never been so glad to finish a race as that one.

March saw the start of regular runs over 10 miles, but even with training limited to five days per week I managed between 50 and 60 miles per week. In this month 234 miles were covered and I began to benefit from this "time-on-my-feet" type of training and at last I began to feel that there might be a chance for me. A 30 kilometre race (18.5 miles) in New Bedford, completed in 2 hours 3 minutes, gave me another opportunity over the longer distances and incidentally to achieve my qualifying time to run the Boston. Although no remarkable advances were shown in my running speed it was significant and heartening that I was still running, albeit slowly and not "out on my feet" as was the case in the "20". There was hope.

On with the training. Towards the end of March each run was over 12 miles but still only 65 miles per week—not enough. It was then that I discovered a new problem, that of boredom. On these runs the first five miles were miserable, the depths of mental depression being reached between five and six miles. After that point mental anguish seemed to recede, until, on the last mile, although I was tired, I was almost happy.

Calculations of running speed in the Boston started to find their way into my thoughts. Consequently I would wear a wristwatch on the runs. This may seem strange to my readers in 2010 where digital watches of extreme complexity are available to everybody. Back in the sixties and seventies stopwatches were like pocket watches, which I could just about hold in the palm of my hand. They were not suitable for long runs. However fast I tried to run I seemed to cover 10 miles in 64 to 65 minutes. After such a training run it would take me two hours to recover—shorter if I was allowed to lie down on a couch with tea and cookies (biscuits) and a good book. A wife and two energetic children prevented this except on one glorious occasion they were out when I returned home after a run and I was allowed to recover in a civilised manner.

Boston is over 300 years old and featured prominently in early American history and was, in 1970, a major port as well as an industrial and academic center (centre). Like so many American cities, it was a chronic sufferer from the multiple ailments of air and water pollution, overcrowding, inadequate public services and increasing social disaffection (if we fast forward to 2010 the above description can be applied to every major city and many minor ones in Great Britain and in Europe).

Boston has superb harbour facilities where the Charles River meets the Atlantic Ocean. Logan International Airport is almost surrounded by water and in 1970 was the eight busiest airport in the world. Around Boston at a distance of 10 miles or so is a three lane expressway, the world-famous Route 128, which in the nineteen fifties and early sixties was the home of some of the most talented industrial expertise in the world. As a result of the 1970's depression the economic outlook is gloomy. Although Route 128 is busy the traffic no longer stops so often at these places, but passes them by.

## The Marathon Organisation

The Boston marathon starts in the small New England town of Hopkinton 26 miles west of Boston. The course leads directly into Boston and the finishing point is at the bottom of the imposing 52-storey skyscraper-type building the Prudential Centre. This tall building, in the heart of downtown Boston, can be seen (smog and pollution permitting) from six miles or so away. The race starts in Haydn Row, a tree-lined street about twenty feet wide. With last year's field greater than 1100 and this year's field being almost the same it can be appreciated that there could be serious congestion at the start.

In previous years anyone was allowed to run and this lead to a prestige-seeking-lunatic fringe on the starting line. None of this fraternity had any intention at all of serious athletic endeavour. The result was of people dropping out from distances of 400 yards from the start and becoming a source of irritation to other competitors, traffic on the road and incidentally to the organisers. For this 1970 race the organisers attempted to limit the field to those who were serious and drew up entry standards, which were not too onerous for serious runners. These were:

1. Completion of two ten mile races, OR
2. Completion of a recognised marathon in under four hours, OR
3. A certificate from a long distance running coach that the candidate had trained adequately.

It was hoped that these measures would cut the entries to manageable proportions. I heard estimates of a reduction by half, but, as it turned out in our race there were 1075 entries and over 1000 actual starters. So with all these runners lined up (and packed deep) in that little narrow street the start itself tended to be a long drawn out affair.

For New Englanders, and particularly Bostonians, this race is a major sporting event—a festive occasion. People have been coming to watch it for years. At work many people were really excited that there was somebody in the company who was actually going to run the Boston Marathon. An interesting aside is the pronunciation of the word "marathon". In Great Britain emphasis is on the first syllable, whereas the New Englanders emphasise the third syllable. A friend told me that there was more publicity in the Boston Media for this race than for the Olympic games. This corroborates other indicators, which suggested that Americans generally were very insular and ignorant of happenings outside their own country.

The Boston marathon (however it is pronounced) starts as has been said, in Hopkinton, and the runners follow Route 135 towards Boston. Once out of this typical and pleasant small New England town the course runs through pleasant undulating open country, with no seriously steep hills. The runners pass through Ashland and Framingham and then onto Natick, where the crossing of Route 27 signifies that the 10-mile point has been reached. Then with stiffening legs the runners press on through to Wellesley, where they join Route 16 and the megalopolis of Boston starts. Wellesley College denotes the halfway point of the marathon (13.1 miles). Soon the 16-mile point is reached when the runners cross Route 128, the Boston ring road. After nearly another mile on Route 16, the runners turn right onto Route 30, Commonwealth Avenue and start the Newton Hills.

The stretch along Commonwealth Avenue, from this junction (17 miles), represents the most severe challenge to the runners. In this four miles are four hills, each about half a mile long. The course took us over the top and along the flat, past the delightful, detached, expansive and expensive-looking houses of the well to do to see the road drop gently away to the right, trees on either side as though the summit of the mountain has been reached. Finally to completely demoralise the runner comes the last, shortest but steepest, hill, which bursts into view when he turns a corner. This leads him up to Boston College. This last hill has been quite correctly named "Heartbreak Hill" and is so-named by newscasters, reporters, broadcasters and all people to whom I spoke after the race. For the runners who reach Boston College, a medieval-type castellated building right at the top of a hill the sight of the finish, seen vaguely through the dirty atmospheric fog across the Boston skyline, is a tonic. The long run in from Boston College along Beacon Street is agony, with the finish coming ever closer, but ever so far away.

## Long Distance Training

Long distance training for this marathon (runs of 14 miles or so) was finished a week before the race. My race plan for that last week was to reduce distances on consecutive runs and to have three days' rest before the race, just to settle the body. In this way I hoped to derive the utmost long-term benefit for the latter stages of the race. The thought in my mind at this time was one of tacit acceptance, reluctantly though, of the necessity to go into the race with just to finish as the main driving force. This was completely against my principles. I had always had some goal, either the clock, or a specific competitor. Now it was just not to be beaten by fatigue. Tentatively I set 65 minutes for ten miles, Boston College in about 2 hours 20 minutes and hoped for three hours or so for my final time.

The few days before the race were sunny and getting steadily warmer. On the day before the race the sky was clear and the temperature in the high 50's (Fahrenheit). So relatively warm and dry was it that I had viewed with some distaste the thought of running it. Fortunately, on race day the wind was from the west, i.e. would be behind the runners on race day.

## **The Race Itself**

At last April 20th dawned and to my joy it was overcast (I wanted rain). But there had been a change in the wind—now from the east. We would have a headwind all the way. Pre-race publicity and the published list of runners gave every indication that the race itself would be a classic—with seven men who had run the distance in under 2 hours 15minutes and that it could be close. The pre-race favourite was the Canadian Jerome Drayton with a best time of 2h 11m 13s, with England's Ron Hill 41 seconds behind, as the expected challenger.

I begged a lift to Hopkinton in the car of a local runner and we arrived at the gymnasium of the Hopkinton Junior

High School where we had to report and to change. In the large gym the highly polished floor was crowded with runners wearing ·all the colours imaginable, the pungent smell of embrocation invading the nostrils. I collected the envelope containing my two numbers (to be pinned on front and back) and the necessary safety pins and a ticket to be attached to my bag for transportation to the end of the race in Boston.

When I came out among the last of the runners to be bussed to the start, the drizzle had given way to heavy rain. I was then glad of my two T-shirts, topped by a long sleeved jersey and my club vest on top. In addition I wore regulation shorts, "regulation" being defined as "as short as possible without actually being indecent."

I took my place in the last line of runners at the start. A husky young man leaned over to me and asked, "What time are you going to do?"

"Oh, about three hours or so," I replied, "Somewhere around there. I'll take it easy to start with."

He thought for a moment. "When is it best to go?" he asked.

I looked blank.

"How far do you go before speeding up?"

"Oh, I'll go slow for 8 to 10 miles, but I think you'll find that once you reach that point, your pace is set. You a runner?" I asked, noticing his fat cheeks and plump arms.

"No, no." he replied thoughtfully.

I jumped up as high as I could, looking ahead towards the start line, but all I could see were the backs of heads, and still more heads.

At last there was a hush, a pause, then only the sound of shuffling feet and then the crack, rather than the bang of the starter's gun. We were off, but around me nothing happened, nobody stirred. I tried to look up front, but all I could see were multi-coloured running vests and the backs of heads. Then, when I had convinced myself that it was a false alarm, runners immediately in front of me shuffled forward and then I was off.

Down Hayden Row we jogged, a mass of shuffling bodies, between the rows of clapping people. We were turned to the right of the truck, which was festooned with cameras and TV crews. We were well and truly off. A cheerful motley we were, spreading right across the road. When the road dipped, it was possible to see through the drenching rain the backs of the heads of the tide of runners. It was cold.

"No running on the right—that's illegal," shouted a young runner as I passed him." After three miles I saw the first casualty—a dark-haired runner limping by the side of the road. Then I felt a stabbing pain at the back of my right knee.

"Oh, no, not now," I thought.

By six miles the pain had moved up the back of my leg and by eight miles it had moved round to the front. By nine miles it had disappeared. Was it just nerves?

An odd assortment we runners must have looked, wearing a collection of bright colours and very odd clothing. Some runners wore plastic bags with holes for arms and heads over varieties of hats and clothing. Some wore just athletics shorts and singlet—some wore hats, gloves, trousers, sweaters. I saw one Vietnam jungle hat, cut down jeans, sweatsuits, athletic strip, woollen hats, woollen gloves and so on.

The occasional groups of people by the side of the road kept up a continuous clapping as we ran by. Sometimes spectators would stand in the road, each spectator standing just a little further out from the kerb than the man or woman next to him, both to see the runners and to hand out a beaker or cup containing drinks. The space available for running narrowed. Children by the side of the road handed out orange pieces. I grabbed one—wonderful—it tasted good.

We passed through Natick, the ten-mile point, where Route 27 crossed the course. A feeding station had been constructed of boards on trestles. The road immediately past it was strewn with plastic or compressed cardboard beakers, dashed to the ground after the runners had taken a swift drink. The road surface glistened. The wind was cold on my face and the rain came down. "Now on to Wellesley Square, the next checkpoint." I muttered to myself. The thought of not finishing the race never crossed my mind.

A group of runners, chatting amicably, came up from behind.

"Real English weather this," shouted a runner I knew as he appeared at my right shoulder. He wore a handkerchief as a headband round his forehead.

"We seem to have picked up quite a crowd," said a tall loping young man.

"Anyone want any ice to suck?" asked the longhaired sickly-faced youth on my left after he had scooped up a beaker of ice from an accomplice waiting by the side of the road. I shook my head in shocked disbelief and my thumbs and fingers ached with the cold. The tall blond runner on my left leaned over, "Yes please," he said.

"I wouldn't mind a bit, if I could," I said, holding out my hand, not wanting to be left out.

"Here," said my benefactor.

The ice went into my mouth, but not for long. "Very good ain't it?" asked the sickly—faced youth. I grinned feebly and nodded.

In the front row of this group of eight or nine runners a bearded red-cheeked runner was holding forth. "You know, when I did my two hours 52 minutes I did one hour forty for the first half and then speeded up. My last eight was in six-minute miles."

"Really," replied his eager listeners. At last we reached Wellesley Square, the halfway point, came up and my time was one hour thirty minutes exactly.

The group slowly pulled away from me and there was nothing I could do about it. "Where is Route 128 my next checkpoint?" I said to myself. Our route passed over a large dual carriageway. "Is that it?" I asked myself, looking eagerly ahead of me trying to find the landmarks I knew." But everything was strange to me, so I had to go on.

"Do you know where Route 128 is?" I asked an elderly balding runner as I passed him." I don't know," he replied. And then he lifted up his arm pointed ahead and said, "Look, there it is." I had not seen the large green sign whose white lettering denoted the entrance to the expressway.

Onto the bridge over the expressway now, (the race time was one hour fifty four minutes, shown on a large race clock on a church wall). We had run 16 miles—only ten miles to go.

"Ron Hill's running away with it, Barry," shouted Graham from the side. Shortly afterwards I heard an excited shout from Lee from work. "Go, go, Barry," he shouted. Out of the corner of my eye I glimpsed his multi-coloured sweater. I suffered in silence.

We ran on past the hospital and I began to feel a bit better. A large piece of orange was handed to me by a bespectacled stout middle-aged man wearing a trilby hat and a raincoat buttoned up to the neck, and seemed to give me new life. I actually enjoyed eating it. At the traffic lights I turned right onto Route 30 and saw the first hill—and the single file of runners straggling across the road to take the left hand bend on the other side of the road.

"Just run you bastard, just run." I said to myself as I saw two runners in front of me who had started to walk. I closed my eyes and plodded on.

"Well done, Barry, "said Ed as he steamed by—he always seemed to pass me on the latter stages of the long races.

"Got to get to Boston College," I said to myself.

The rain still came down and it was still cold.

Some time later at the top of a hill, "What's that in front?—It's Boston College. It can't be. Where was the second hill?" I had not noticed it, so wrapped up as I was with the running. On the top of the hill by the College I passed the lines of students who were clapping (the 21 mile point). "Tell me, was that Boston College?" I asked the runner on my left shoulder. He nodded, "Yes," he gasped. I had run further than I had ever run before.

I was exhilarated. "I've made it. I can drop out any time I like now." Now I was running faster down the long gradient. Our side of the road was covered with stones and the other side of the road was roped off for excavations. But I was tired and hurting all over.

At the left turn into Beacon Street (22 miles) I received the shock of my life. A yellow vest moved up on my left and I looked and looked again. The contoured chest silhouette denoted female companionship. She wore jeans cut off below the knee and a yellow jersey. "I'll never live it down," I thought. "Oh, well if she's good enough to get this far she's good enough to beat me in." Male chauvinism was then in vogue and women did not normally run marathons. I forced myself to run harder and she dropped back out of sight.

Now the long drawn-out run down Beacon Street—it was interminable. I looked at the house numbers, and saw number 1175.

"Is that the Prudential Building in front?" I thought. At last we crossed into Commonwealth Avenue. Half a mile to go! In front was a plantation of yellow jackets worn by the traffic police.

"Down there is where we turn," I thought. No, the bloody runners are going past there. Where is the finish?"

There they go—streaking right—flashes of colour against the dark backcloth of the spectators.

"Go on, Barry," a voice I knew from work. With the turning into Hereford Street about 30 yards away and the finish, or so I thought, just around the corner, I sprinted into the corner, leaned into it, kicked coming out of it. But the finish was nowhere in sight. I kept my legs going, my heart pounding, my chest burning. We staggered up the rise to the Prudential Building, crossed Boylston Street, which was roped off. Then we turned left down a long hill, which ended in the forecourt of the Prudential Building where the finish line came into view. I tried to sprint again and—then it was all over. I heard the blood pounding in my ears. I noticed the spectators looking at me and the other runners with a mixture of reverence, awe and curiosity.

It was all over. When we crossed the finish line we stepped into the front door of the Prudential building and onto an escalator, which took us up to the shopping plaza. On our left was a rope, the other side of which stood the ranks of eager spectators, young and old, male and female, looking puzzled and excited.

We walked about forty yards along the shopping plaza, the crowd to our left and a 12 foot or so high plate-glass window on our right, through which we could see the ornamental ponds of the Centre and the buildings of downtown Boston. Then we were guided into the metal-door of the elevator (lift) which took us up to the first (second) floor to the showers (In America there is no "ground" floor and you walk off the street through the front door into the First Floor. To the American the floor above is the second floor, but to the Englishman this is the first floor. Long live the ambiguity of the English language.) Maybe my attitude showed because in work I was once referred to as "That Goddam Englishman" which pleased me no end.

## Afterwards

"Where's the shower?" I asked of the haggard, shattered, barely recognisable, figure of a runner I knew.

"Over there," he mouthed, turning his head towards an open doorway in the wall on the other side of the room.

I stripped off my wet clothes, took my towel from my bag and picked my way through crowds of half-clothed men to the open doorway. A sad-looking trio passed in front of me. One of the Japanese runners, a tall, well-built young man, grey blanket draped loosely around his shoulders, was being helped by two men, one Japanese, one American, to drag his lifeless body across the room. His agonised eyes stared hopelessly into space. His feet shuffled helplessly on the floor.

I entered the steam-filled room in which I could vaguely see through twenty or so naked or semi-naked bodies. From a doorway at the other end of the room belched clouds of steam and the sound of running water. Through the doorway all I could see was heads.

"Where's the shower, John?" I asked a grey-haired man I knew, who was towelling himself down. "In there, Barry." He said, inclining his head towards the doorway," but there's only two. I'm not waiting. How did it go?"

"Oh. OK, I finished." I grinned, "I don't know the time."

I had my shower, dried myself and then went back to my first friend, still sitting where I had left him, still staring helplessly into space. I shivered and I noticed that everyone was shivering. You could almost hear the "Symphony for Chattering Teeth". It had been cold and we had to warm up.

I then remembered the flask of hot, sweet, milky coffee, which I had in my bag, but also felt the icy tentacles of exposure, which were reaching all through my body. I had to get some clothes on—and then drink the coffee. The odour of the coffee soon reached the nostrils of my immediate neighbours, so in response to mute appeals the coffee disappeared into several stomachs.

I finished dressing, ate my apple and then searched in my bag for my watch. It was.

3.38pm. So, I had run the race in round about 3 hours ten minutes. Later I received a certificate which stated that I finished 363rd in 3 hours 9 minutes 44 seconds.

"How about some stew, Barry?" shouted Bob. I nodded. We got into the lift—the only way out to the changing rooms being used by the runners. On the floor above we pushed out of the elevator (lift), only to find ourselves in a five foot wide corridor, with backs of heads stretching up to a corner about ten feet away and then to another corner, a further fifteen feet away. This we could see by means of a "fish eye" mirror hanging on the wall at the first corner. A wait in the corridor took us to the counter behind which white coated staff ladled out stew from a large stainless steel tub into white bowls, hot steaming stew which smelled wonderful. It was delicious—chunky, thick creamy gravy—bags of body for deserving athletes.

A weary day was finished off by the realisation that at 5.30pm I had to catch the bus to return home. The results were posted for those fast enough to finish inside 2 hours 55 minutes and 220 had done that. The statistics of this race make interesting reading.

It was won by Ron Hill in 2 hours 10 minutes 30 seconds, a new course record.

4 runners finished in less than 2 hours 15 minutes.
6 runners finished in less than 2 hours 20 minutes.
31 runners finished in less than 2 hours 30 minutes.
81 runners finished in less than 2 hours 40 minutes
The first woman finished in 3 hours 5 minutes.
5 women finished the race.
Nearly eleven hundred runners started the race.

I would like to end this account with a tribute to the organisers of the race, without whose efforts nothing would have been accomplished and also those representatives of faceless mediocrity—the runners. Most are never in the medals, the prizewinners or the honours lists. I am of course one of these and am constantly reminded of their individual battles, equally as courageous and individually as stimulating and rewarding as those of the champions. I would like to leave the reader with the observation that the ecstasy of finishing almost compensates for the agony of the running.

END

# CHAPTER 6

# A CUMBRIAN TSUNAMI—LUNCHTIME RUN

For most of my adult life I have been a competitive runner and training consists of going out for runs, five days a week or more. Most runners fit their training in whenever and wherever they can during their working day. When I travelled on business the first items I packed into my suitcase would be my running kit. In my hotel, in another country maybe, I would change into shorts and running vest or other appropriate clothing, go down in the lift, through the hotel lobby and out into a sometimes-crowded city street. I was always aware of the constant danger of getting lost and to prevent this my practice was to turn left outside the front door and continue to turn left until I returned to my starting point. Mostly this worked well but on occasions my return would be delayed.

Runners often have busy schedules and I advise them to search their working day to find pockets of time in which they can run. Most people squander time, often without realising it and the most inefficient use of time in the day occurs in the period between waking up and actually going to work. This period can be utilised by having running clothing close to the bed or the outside door so that they can get up, change into running gear and slip out of the door all in one movement. They then wake up a mile or so down the road. The run must be gentle and it works. The run oxygenates the blood and you start the day feeling alive and able to concentrate well right from the start. Other suitable periods in the day are lunchtime (one hour needed), evenings (early or late) or during the day when you are away from the office and a Leisure Centre or running track or park is available. Sometimes it is possible to drive into a parking area by the side of the road, change in the car and then run on strange roads in the countryside and this approach is sometimes adopted by salesmen or marketing runners I have known.

Early in my adult life I was going to night school on four nights a week and at the weekends I was competing and studying. The only time I could find to train in the week was in the lunchtime, and this became my preferred training time. I would often meet up with other runners, sometimes from the same company or at the local track or park. After the run I would have a shower where possible before returning to work but on occasions when these were not available, would use the hand basins in the gentlemen's washrooms to wash hands, face and feet so as to freshen up for the afternoon work period.

In the late eighties I was employed in the commercial department of a large engineering company in the North

West of England and continued to run at lunchtimes, in addition to other times of day when possible. As usual I had persuaded other athletes to run with me and used my car to drive us to the local track on Walney Island and back. My car was an elderly second-hand red Fiat 126, which I had seen by the side of the main road into work with a For Sale notice—£400. This eye-catching heap of metal was irreverently named the "Basmobile" by Kevin. It was the subject of much ribald and sarcastic comments by many people both within and outside the department. This car was a "mini" in the true meaning of the word and when I parked it towards the front of a standard parking space in the company car park I was often asked why I hadn't brought my trailer into work that day because there was enough space behind the Fiat for a trailer of the same size and both would still stay within the designated parking spot. The car itself could just about take four large (some very large) adults and often did. From the track we would run, shower back at the track and get back for work afterwards, all within the lunch hour (occasionally with some slight stretching of time scales).

As part of a company reorganisation our department was to be re-housed in a new building and I was tasked with laying out our new offices and therefore for a while became the most powerful man in the department. "Barry, can I have more power points here?" "Barry, can you build my office to include a window," etc. It occurred to me that I might be able to use this new power to my "running" advantage, because I worked on this project with Ron Jenkins, the senior manager with overall responsibility for layout of the whole building.

"Ron," I said one day, "in the new toilets can we have some showers installed? If we put them in at the design stage the increase in costs will be minimal." After some consideration he liked the idea and agreed and after some months, we ended up with a very good shower in the gents toilet. An interesting consequence of this redesign of the plumbing was that because the men had a shower in their toilets the women must have one in their toilets. I thought this a good idea, because then two of us could shower at the same time, one of us using the women's shower. However I had not realised the impossibility of men's entering the ladies' toilets, even if there were no ladies there at the time. Of course when they were installed the ladies' showers were used regularly (by women of course). However with a shower in our building we were able to run straight from our building and had more flexibility in distances we were able to run in the time available.

One day, after a hectic morning's work, Chris, Kevin and I grabbed our sports bags from under our desks and hurried to the Fiat. We drove through the main gate to the running track, where we changed and set off on our run. We had a variety of circuits, each of about 30 minutes maximum duration, the choice on the day being arbitrary. Usually we did not repeat the course we had run the day before. Soon after we started Kevin turned off onto a shorter run and Chris and I decided on the coast run, which went towards and along the beach, and up onto a coastal walk which formed part of the sea defences on that side of the island. The surface was about five metres wide and on the right hand side was a rock wall, which provided an additional sea defence. In high tides, with strong winds driving the sea, the seawater would crash over the walkway, hit the wall and drain back into the sea. As usual I wore shorts and T-shirt, my new high technology vari-vu spectacles and a cloth cap to keep out the sun's rays. This was in the era before baseball caps became commonplace in this country for runners.

At the beach Chris was thirty metres or so in front, gradually increasing his lead with every stride, as usual. We ran hard along the rocky walkway, the sea on our left, and the rocky wall on our right. As I looked left I could see the white horses as far as the eye could see all the way to the horizon, driven by a strong gusting wind. It was approaching high tide. Looking ahead to the sea wall I saw that the tide nearly reached the top of the wall, the sea lapping just to the top of the walkway and occasionally over onto the top. Chris was about two hundred metres in front when he joined the walkway and I saw him run smoothly along the top to the other end before he turned right and disappeared from view. He was a stronger runner than I and this was normal practice and I was not unduly disturbed by his disappearance.

When I was about fifty yards into the walkway I glanced left and saw a long single large wave stretching from behind me then in front of me, as far as I could see towards the horizon, moving across in front of me, peacefully and smoothly. I was about one hundred metres along the walkway, with another two hundred yards to go to where I would turn right inland, away from the coast. The wave started to lap over the walkway behind me and overtook me, a rolling torrent of water spreading over the concrete. It crashed over the walkway and into the rock wall and catapulted back towards the sea. I was completely submerged as the wave hit the walkway, bounced right over me, seemed to push me forward and simultaneously I was pushed hard towards the rock wall on my right. For some strange reason I did not fall over. Then I felt the returning water grab hold of my legs below the knees and try to pull my feet from under me towards the edge of the walkway into the turbulent frothing whirl-pooling sea water, about ten feet deep at that point. I slipped, fell down but managed to hold onto some projections on the uneven floor of the walkway and held myself there as the water receded. I picked myself up, totally drenched, stumbled forwards into a jog, then into a run through the frothing bubbling seawater, hearing in my imagination the angry cries of the demons of the deep at allowing a victim to escape. I reached the other end of the walkway, before turning round and looking out to sea. The white horses were there. The sea was just lapping over the walkway but there was no sign of any large wave, no sign of anything untoward. It had been a one-off early tsunami, decades before the name would be better-known to the world.

I looked up and realised that I couldn't read the name on the nearby street sign and the caravans on the nearby site were blurred.

"Am I going blind?" I thought, starting to panic. I looked down at my hands, noticing that my fingers were white, standard for me in cold conditions. In a reflex action I brushed my hand up across my face to run my fingers through my hair and realised that my spectacles and my cap had gone, the spectacles probably to the bottom of the sea, my cap probably on its way to Ireland, eighty or so miles away.

The sun was shining, the wind was fresh and I could see to run the mile back to the track, where Chris and Kevin met me.

"Where have you been?" asked Chris.

"You should have waited to have a shower here," said Kevin sarcastically, looking at my sodden shorts and T-shirt, now drying out. My reply was terse and probably unprintable. Fortunately, to cater for my long-established ability to lose things and to break things I always carried a second pair of distance spectacles, which I used for driving, and a second pair of reading spectacles. I had bought these shortly after buying the vari-focals purely because wearing the vari-focals made my eyes tired.

In the car going back to work I told them what had happened and they realised how close it had been. Chris had not experienced anything untoward and Kevin hadn't been there. By the time we rolled the Basmobile back into its parking place, fifteen minutes later than usual, we were back to normal, ready for the afternoon's work, but to make matters worse I had left my sandwiches at home that day. I was hungry that afternoon, a condition which made the afternoon longer than usual for me.

The next day I ordered a new pair of spectacles from the optician and thought about what had happened. I decided to claim for them on my household insurance policy. The result would depend on the insurance company's definition of "lost", or would they have argued that the spectacles were damaged? I didn't know. I still have a copy of my insurance claim and I feel sure it would have been read with amusement in the Claims office of the insurance company. Whatever happened, three weeks later I received a cheque for £97, being £85 for the spectacles and £12 for the cap, for both of which items I was able to provide receipts, having bought them shortly beforehand.

Lunchtime runs are rarely as eventful as the one described above.

END

# CHAPTER 7

# A SCRUBBER'S VIEWPOINT—THE 1973 MAXOL MARATHON

A "scrubber" in running terms means a runner who usually finishes towards the back of the field in races and usually comprises the old, overweight, injured, has-beens, etc. With typical English inverted humour, in one famous club, Thames Valley Harriers (TVH), the term "Scrubber" referred to an elite few, usually of international calibre, whose vests had embroidered on the front a drawing of a scrubbing brush. However in this story I qualified as a genuine scrubber.

Most race reports are biased towards an elite few, those athletes who over the years have turned their bodies into ruthlessly efficient machines and became well known, across the Athletics world, far away from their geographical haunts. These men dominated the athletics scene and could churn out miles faster than five minutes for the major part of a marathon (26.2 miles or 42.2 kilometres), before either dominating or being ruthlessly crushed by a "Better-on the-Day" man. A far cry it is to the 6 minutes 35 seconds per mile I achieved for over 22 miles in this race before being reduced to a shambling hulk by the last 4 miles, or 6 minutes 50 seconds per mile overall. Or is it? This report is written by one of those faceless competitors who finished the race long after the winner and leading bunch had finished and when the media representatives had moved on to their next assignment. It is written in the hope that it will provide light entertainment and a different slant to normal.

On the day of the race I was 38 years old, married, wife, two boys (aged 5 and 6) mortgage, garden etc, Electronics Engineer by profession. Fitness? I had run regularly over the years but was slowing down. We had moved around the world a bit. I had no great performances to my credit; in fact quite a few mediocre ones. My only marathon to date before this one was the Boston in 1970 in which I ran 3 hours 9 minutes 44 seconds. Over the last six months before the Maxol Marathon in Manchester I had achieved an unprecedented (for me) 50 miles per week. In contrast to the top runners, about whom it is said, "They weigh every cornflake and time every mad dash to the loo," I have tended to eat more or less what I felt like and what my one-time ulcers would allow. My dual aims in the Maxol were firstly to finish and secondly to do so in under three hours. I considered that my training was good enough for that.

My pre-Maxol build-up was supposed to include the Finchley 20, but I lost my car keys on the morning of the race and didn't make the start. I had intended to run the Chichester to Portsmouth 16 mile road race but my team manager wanted me to run in a track League Match, so I missed that one too. So, in desperation and needing a race before the marathon I ran the Maidenhead 10—finishing in 62 minutes exactly, 17 seconds faster than when I last ran over the same course fourteen years previously in 1960. Over that last six weeks hard training for the Maxol my weekly mileage climbed from 45 to 74. The longest continuous run was 18 miles—the longest in one day was 19 miles (lunchtime and evening). My last hard training day was 10 days before the race, while the last easy training day was 4 days before. My intention was to run 40 minutes per 10,000 metres from the start and see what happened.

So, after pre-race nerves having extended over the best part of a week, I joined the coach at Lincolns Inn Fields on the Saturday and immediately met old friends who were also running this marathon. As usual on such occasions, discussion ranged over Athletics, particularly road running, form, hopes, aches and pains, etc. In Manchester we were dropped with the others at the YMCA in Alexandra Park, where we stayed the night. After a meal at which conversation was again on Athletics, Marathon running, personalities, training methods, future hopes and past performances, etc. I joined a group to go out for a beer. We walked out into Princess Street and by instinct turned left towards Manchester. There were six of us, all a little tensed up.

After walking some way we stopped at a bus stop to ask a man, "Where's the nearest pub, mate?" The man pointed back the way we had come and said "Down that street there." He paused. Then, as he moved forward to catch his bus, he added, "but you'll get hassled by spades in there." With that cryptic remark he got onto the bus and his further remarks were lost as the engine revved up and the bus moved away.

By common consent we walked across the road to the street the woman had indicated. John muttered thoughtfully, "Never heard that one before. If we have a bad one tomorrow we can always say we were hassled by spades." It relieved the tension. So did the beer. As alcohol flowed spirits soared and tongues loosened. As intended times for tomorrow were discussed I rediscovered something I had uneasily felt at the dinner table. I was not within 20 minutes of the slowest of them. I wondered if I would have any company at all in the race. At 9.30pm we returned to the YMCA, stopping at a fish and chip shop staffed by Chinamen. We ordered portions of chips, which served to build up our carbohydrates.

Back in my room on the top floor the silence was interrupted each minute by a resounding "Kladonk" as the hand on clock on the wall clock outside my room moved on. I got all my gear out for the morrow. I tried on my shoes—fairly new—should I or shouldn't I wear them? They felt comfortable. Which shorts, the new tight-round-the waist—or the old and tatty but comfortable pair. I chose the latter. I walked around the room, simulating my final sprint for the tape. All appeared well. So I put everything back into my bag, got into my bed and read my book until I felt myself on the comfortable gradual slope into dreamland. I closed the book, turned out the light and laid my head on the pillow. But sleep was elusive that night.

No sooner had I put my head on the pillow when sounds broke through the feeble senses of my hearing system, made doubly sensitive by pre-race nerves. It seemed as though the return pipe for the plumbing went just by my room and it was noisy continuously. People marched along the corridor to their rooms and shouted their "goodnights" as though on a parade ground. However, I drifted off to sleep, to be woken up yet again at 4.30am. From then until 7.10 am when I felt it was a reasonable time to wake up, I seemed to be only half-asleep.

Down to breakfast at 7.25am—what a lovely sight. I grabbed my choices—cornflakes, two slices of toast (pity no marmalade), hard-boiled egg, cup of coffee (later to be supplemented by a second). At the tables were runners, some already track-suited. But they were outnumbered by packets—of wheat germ, glucose, dextrose, etc. I had brought along blackcurrant squash, to which I added hot water. By 7.50am I felt quite full and really pleasantly determined to give it a real go. Then I took a walk outside to gauge the weather—terribly important. It would probably rain.

The bus took us to the start, by the YMCA in St. Peter's Square where I collected my numbers and yellow plastic bag for our tracksuits. Then we went down through the judo dojo to the inner changing room. Very carefully I got my things out. An Irishman tried to provoke comment by remarking on the atmosphere, the dressing room, the race, but nobody took him on. Conversation was subdued. Which vest—extra T-shirt or not? A quick walk outside decided me in favour of a singlet, a wise decision as it turned out.

Just before 10am the crowd of athletes gathered on the inner island of the square. The pavements were crowded. The announcer said, ". . . . International Marathon . . . . competitors from nine countries . . . Put tracksuits into the yellow bags. Leave them on the pavement . . . . They will be picked up later." There was an uneasy shuffling while the athletes lined up. After a short, intense silence the starter fired his gun and we were off.

As we left the square I glanced over my shoulder to see only three runners behind me. I felt a twinge of pain in my right little toe. My mouth was dry. "I should have drunk more water," I thought. I ambled along and after about two miles I moved up to Bernard and colleagues from Manchester, who had supporters all the way along. They talked about their three-hour target, so why not stick together. I explained my plan, to run 40 minutes per 10k which, if maintained would result in a time of about 2 hours 49 minutes. But we would slow down in the later parts of the race. At the 5km marker a timekeeper shouted "20 minutes 17 seconds," as I passed.

"Beautiful pace," I said to myself. "Must keep this going till the 10km," I said out loud. I had spent a long time familiarising myself with the map and had split the race into four 10km sections and then the final 2.2km to the finish. The course took the runners three times round an accurate 10k loop and then a larger loop to the finish.

The rain started soon after the 5km marker—warm steady rain. Some people gave support from the pavements, some stared at us through front room windows. The 10km marker came up "41 minutes 18", shouted a timekeeper. "Look Bernard. We're a bit slow. I think we ought to wind it up a bit, now," I said. I increased the pace a little and he came with me, but on a slight downhill of the dual carriageway he fell behind. At about 12km I needed a toilet so ran into a garage. As I stood on the toilet floor I felt my right big toe throbbing—blast those shoes. Off again—and I chased the red-vested runner I had passed a little way back. I was running easily and gaining on the runners ahead. A little while later I recognised the green vest of Worthing AC "All right, Ian?" I said as I passed him. He shouted something in reply and I went on. Towards the end of the loop I felt a tickle just below and behind my left knee. It seemed to drift slowly down my calf and then to explode. It was painful. "This is it." I said to myself. I eased off and tried to favour the leg by limping. Mortification set in. "I can't go back and say that I dropped out at 11 miles," I thought. I shall have to enter the Poly (Polytechnic marathon) just to get a time." Then, miraculously, the pain seemed to recede.

Much to my surprise, over this period I did not seem to lose much ground.

With the 20km going by in 81 minutes 18seconds, my second 10k was completed in exactly 40 minutes, right on schedule. Now for the third lap, i.e. the second loop. I was feeling quite good and steadily making up ground on the field. Just after the 21km feeding station at which (like other runners), I had refused all offers of refreshment, so energetically made by many young people. The pain in my right big toe increased. I had to do something. I stopped, knelt down and undid my shoe. I pulled some loose foam rubber from underneath my heel and wrapped it round the offending toe. I laced up the shoe again. I felt more than heard the recovery vehicle stop. I looked up towards the windscreen and shook my head vehemently. Damned impertinence! Off again, but oh, the legs were stiff. All right. Ease off a little—hold it for a while and wait for the runners ahead to start to come back to me. It was the Worthing runner again. "Had toe trouble Ian," I said as I passed him.

Towards the end of the second loop the rain stopped and the sun came out. Then just before a roundabout, which marked the end of the loop, I was suddenly turned off the road along a roped-off path around a building site. Just for a moment I stopped, not knowing where to go, before being shouted at by a spectator, who pointed the way to rejoin the course. This diversion had not been there the first time round and was presumably caused by traffic congestion at the roundabout. I was tired but the 30km point came up at 2h 2m 45s. Incredible! I was amazed to be running at the same speed, though the effort to this do was much greater than before. Now we were obviously back inside the Manchester city boundary. I passed the 35-kilometre marker in 2 hours 23 minutes 11 seconds, still on schedule. My mind was still calculating "That's 20 minutes 11 seconds plus 15 seconds gives me 20 minutes 26 for the last 5k. If I keep this up I'll have 2h 53s or so."

At the 36k feeding station I took my first drink—a beaker of orange squash. I drank a mouthful, washed my mouth out with another and threw the beaker away. Now I was passed by red vest. I was tiring and the floodlights of Old Trafford appeared on my left and finally I turned a corner and there it was. The finish was in there and a long line of runners was approaching from the other direction and turning across my line of run into the stadium. Then I passed the entrance and I knew I had to go on. I recognised Dave coming the other way and he was strained about the face, as they all were. They were running in the middle of the road, some of them wobbling along. I saw, his straight black hair seemingly plastered down onto his headband he shouted encouragement to me as he ran past me before turning right to finish in the stadium.

Now I felt the wind in my face and felt lonely and despondent. But onward, alongside the railway line. I could see lines of runners, one going out the way I was going, the other coming back towards me, as far down the straight road as far as I could see. "Where's that blasted marker?" I thought. We turned a corner and then I could see in the distance a vivid orange jacket. My heart sank and I thought I would not make it even to him. But of course I did and rounded him to start the long run back. The time at the marker was 2 hours 48 minutes 45 seconds. "Have I dropped all that time? I've lost five minutes. I shan't make three hours. It's two kilometres to go."

But that also passed and suddenly I made the final right turn into the entrance road. Someone shouted, "Two hours fifty seven," and I tried to make my legs go faster but they felt as though they didn't know what they were supposed to do. "I might even do it." I thought. Now we ran off the road and onto the rough gravel at the entrance to the stadium. "Out of my way," I snarled silently at a red-hatted youth who walked across my path giggling at a girl. I staggered and turned down behind the stands only to be turned right underneath the stadium. Inside we turned sharp left turn and a run under the stands brought us finally to a right turn into the entrance tunnel. Coming out of the tunnel I was suddenly in the open air and was turned left onto the narrow right-angled cinder track, which surrounded that well-known Mancunian turf, the Manchester United football pitch at Old Trafford. I was surprised to see that the pitch was raised about a foot above the running track. I glance over my right shoulder, expecting to see the finish across the other side, but panicked, as I couldn't see it. At the first right turn behind the goal line I felt even greater panic, as I still couldn't see the finish. It was then that I realised the malicious cunning of the organisers of the race. The finish was right by the entrance tunnel and we had run a complete circuit to finish. A burly white-vested runner was in front of me and out of the final turn I sprinted past him and then—it was all over.

Some short time later, I heard the announcer say, "Three hours is up," or words to that effect. Although absolutely shattered I was pleased. My actual time was 2 hours 59 minutes, 34 seconds and I was 179th out of 222 finishers. The exhilaration of setting a pb (personal best) and also breaking the three-hour barrier made bearable the training and misfortunes before the race and the largest blood blister of my career under my big toe.

Full credit to the organisation of the Road Runners Club and to the population of Manchester who gave wonderful support on a day whose weather must have daunted all but the most determined. It was wonderful for marathon running but hostile to many other forms of human activity.

June 1973

END

# CHAPTER 8

# THE JOGGING BOOM

The term "Jogging Boom" refers to the spontaneous movement among the general public to run, or to jog (run slowly) and was encouraged by the first London Marathon in 1981. I call this the first jogging boom because much later, in the 21st century the second jogging boom resulted from the public's participation in major races, half marathons and 10k races, all over the world, a major theme of which seemed to be to provide funds for various charities.

In each case the running bug took hold of many people in all walks of life who would not have considered themselves sporting and their major spontaneous desire was to run, the main race attraction being the marathon. The joggers started, as their name implies, to run slowly and then socially. Some joined existing athletics clubs and some started clubs of their own. In established Athletics clubs joggers were welcomed by many but resented by other, seriously competitive club runners. A surprising unintended beneficiary of this jogging boom has been the improved health of the nation because the training each jogger puts in improves his/

her cardio-vascular system and consequently his/her health has reduced visits to the medical professionals. Further benefits may be felt in combating obesity, which at the time of writing will probably become the major killer in western society within the next twenty years.

In the autumn of 1985, at the height of the Jogging Boom, I was an Amateur Athletic Association (A.A.A.) Senior Coach and regularly coached track and cross country runners, mainly from Crawley Athletic Club, the local club. I noticed that on training nights, just outside the entrance to the running track and changing rooms a large group of joggers (mainly men) congregated, milled around and then went out for runs in their own groups. They kept to themselves and did not come onto the track. I felt that from a coaching point of view they were neglected and that they would benefit from using the track, with its exact distances marked and smooth surface.

As an experiment I organised a pilot programme of running for them, on the track. I based the programme on their known strengths, namely that they were all strong runners even if their running speed was low (relatively speaking). I put up a notice advertising the following track programme, to be held on one night per week for a period of five weeks. This would be in addition to their normal running activities.

| WEEK NO | QUANTITY | DISTANCE (METRES) | NO OF LAPS | RECOVERY (METRES JOG) |
|---------|----------|-------------------|------------|------------------------|
| 1 | 16 | 400 | 1 | 100 |
| 2 | 12 | 600 | 1.5 | 200 |
| 3 | 10 | 800 | 2 | 200 |
| 4 | 12 | 600 | 1.5 | 200 |
| 5 | 16 | 400 | 1 | 100 |

I cautioned them that they should run the first 400 metre lap of each session as though they were starting a short road race (of say two miles) but to run it that little bit faster. The recoveries were to be jogged, much slower than the set distance. They were going to run five miles or so on the track, just a little faster than they would normally run. I did not know what to expect. They just needed someone to show interest. The results were as follows:

1. Where I expected them to run 90 to 100 seconds per 400 metres they ran 75 to 85 seconds.
2. They followed my instructions, i.e. they exercised caution on the first one or two repetitions.
3. After the first two runs of the set they maintained a surprisingly high pace. Their bodies seemed to take over and they were able to run the remainder of the session at a constant speed.
4. During the session the runners tended to settle into performance peer groups, which were maintained throughout.
5. By week four, i.e. on the down side of the pyramid, they had improved their average

400 metre running speed by some two to four seconds.

6. They enjoyed the sessions so much that I was required to develop a longer programme for them.

It seemed that the joggers had the benefit of ignorance and did what they were told. It is noteworthy that many of those joggers went on to greater performances at club level. By the time I left Crawley in November 1987 respectable performances had been set by many runners from this group. These performances, taken from my records, are not outstanding in absolute terms and they required much subsequent application by the athletes but the origins were in those sessions. Some of these performances are shown below and names have been omitted to avoid embarrassment.

| ATHLETE | 800 METRES | 3000 METRES STEEPLECHASE | 5000 METRES |
|---------|-----------|-------------------------|-------------|
| A | 1min 58.7secs | | 15min 34 secs |
| B | 2min 02.8secs | 9min 48secs | 16min 15 secs |
| C | | 10min 28secs | 16min 32 secs |
| D | | 10min 48secs | 16min 40 secs |
| E | | 10min 36 secs | 17min 06 secs |

Within that group of joggers was another group who, with much more application proved that they had significant athletic ability, which would not have been demonstrated had they not become part of that jogging group and secondly, in which they were encouraged to extend their abilities. They were then adults, some moving towards middle age and one can only speculate on their eventual performance levels had they been introduced to a structured improvement programme much earlier in life. Ability abounds in most children and they become subject to that "lottery of life" described in Chapter 2. For an example of one talented youngster who left Athletics and returned to it many years later see Chapter 12.

Of great interest to me was the fact that some highly-competitive and highly-motivated track athletes tried this programme but ran too fast at the start and were unable to complete the sessions. However some members of this Monday training group of joggers became highly experienced distance runners who were part of Crawley AC's winning London to Brighton road races in 1987, 1988 and 1989.

The sessions shown above need not be done on a running track. They can be done effectively on road, grass, canal path or forest path, etc. What is needed is intelligent application. The main concept to master is the use of bulk, short recovery sessions. This programme improves aerobic endurance and is more effective than going out for a steady run, the staple diet of any runner's training repertoire.

END

# CHAPTER 9

# RUNNING AND SEX AND BEER

Male runners are probably no different to any other male groups in life or sport from the point of alleged sexual prowess or ability. On this subject, but from a practical viewpoint, many years ago in a room in Berkshire, some runners gathered to discuss recent training, races coming up and the usual discussion points when runners meet. However on this occasion the subject sex came up and its effect on training and followed a joking reference one married man to another, "You don't look too good, Don. Too long on the nest last night, Eh?" said Alan. Don laughed, as one does, grinned and then said, "Well how many times before training then?" There was laughter all round and then discussions started. After various suggestions, ribald and serious, one of the older and possibly more worldly wise men, suggested, "Well it seems to me that if you have it once, no trouble with any training session the next day. You need about four hours between getting your leg over after a hard training run. If you have it twice in the night, just go out for an easy run. If you have it three times that night, don't run at all the next day." There was laughter, subdued at first, then rolling round the room as everybody joined in the amused acceptance of this verdict from the voice of experience.

But always stories abound and it may be that there could be another powerful basic motivation for the jogging boom, described in Chapter 8, namely the possibility of improving sexual prowess, particularly in men. This could be coupled with the great success and interest in running marathons. In the male chauvinist world, sexual prowess is often exaggerated and anecdotal and in the early 1980's, the time of the jogging boom, stories suggesting this were doing the rounds. As always with such stories it was always, "A fellow I knew", or "A friend of mine," or "This chap . . ." However, as the story goes, two male runners belonging to a well-known athletic club got married on the same day and decided to spend their honeymoons with their respective spouses in the same hotel. They were very competitive athletes, John being a marathon runner, Sid's events being 800/1500 metres. As part of their nuptial celebrations they had agreed a bet on which of them could have sex more times on their wedding night. It was not disclosed if their spouses were aware of these arrangements.

The couples were duly married and after the formal send offs by their respective families they arrived at the designated hotel, having booked adjacent rooms. Sid was a teacher, very organised and in preparation for the night's activities, had brought with him from school three sticks of chalk, one green, one blue and one red. John was an engineer and had not brought anything special.

After booking into the hotel they retired to their respective rooms and Sid soon started his amorous intentions with his new wife, who was equally enthusiastic. They rolled apart triumphantly some time later, pleased with their efforts. Sid was pleased with his wife's reactions and pleased that he had started on his attempt to win his bet. He was a betting man and did not like to lose, either a bet, a horse race, or a track race. He reached into his briefcase which he had put by the side of his bed and withdrew the green chalk and marked a vertical line on the headboard just above his pillow. He replaced the chalk in his brief case and caressed his wife. After resting a while he gently stroked his wife's arm, then her neck and then, with her cheerful acceptance, started his second intercourse coupling. After frenzied and sweaty activity he slowly lifted his body and rolled over to lie beside her, both of them perspiring freely but pleasantly sleepy and satisfied. He put his hand into his briefcase again and withdrew the blue chalk and drew another vertical line on the headboard next to the green chalk mark already there. They then both drifted off to sleep.

Some time later, Sid woke slowly, driven by the competitive drive to win the bet. He gently woke his wife, who murmured in her half-asleep state but soon joined his rhythmic movements until after their climax he slid off her and rested face down on the sheet, his free arm draped protectively over her now-bare stomach. He forced himself to get up, find the red chalk from his briefcase and then make another vertical stroke next to the green and blue marks already there. They both drifted off into a deep sleep.

They were woken by a scratching on their door, followed by slow, repeated knocks. Sid got up slowly from the bed, staggered painfully to the door, which he opened to see John leaning heavily onto the doorframe. John looked dreadful, his eyes bloodshot, his normally thin face even more gaunt than normal, his damp pyjama top hanging loosely around his shoulders. He opened his mouth to say something, stuttered and then looked past Sid's shoulder and saw the three vertical chalk marks on the headboard. "Oh, Christ, Sid, a hundred and eleven. You fit bastard. You beat me by one."

It is just possible that this story circulated around the jogging fraternity and athletic clubs and may have been instrumental in more joggers being interested in running marathons on the road than 800's and 1500's on the track.

I have found that runners, like so many men, in and outside sport, like their beer, or other tipple. However my experience with runners is they prefer beer as opposed to wines or spirits. Here the word "beer" includes lagers, strong and weaker real ales and most runners in my experience are not into wines or spirits. This habit extends far into the elite performers and I know of at least one ex-world record holder who regularly drank heavily before and after races. I believed and practised my belief that a six mile run the morning after was the ideal cure for a hangover. In the modern running world, some scientists and medical professionals suggest that abstinence or at least sensible drinking should be observed. Some have even suggested that alcohol should be declared a banned substance for all sportsmen. I disagree totally with this view. I have observed that longer distance runners, (5K track runners and above) show a sound ability to drink fairly heavily, with no ill effects, in so doing utilising the high energy content of the beer to fuel their energy requirements of being on their feet for extended periods.

To illustrate this point in the late 1990's I was a member of Barrow & Furness Striders Athletic Club and, like other organisations in the town, the Executive Committee had arranged a visit to Hartley's Brewery in Ulverston, just nine miles along the A590 towards the M6 motorway. At that time I had been with the club for about two years and was actively coaching a number of male runners, who finished high up in cross country and road races. Some of them also ran marathons. The visit to the Brewery had been arranged some eighteen months previously and the waiting time was probably an indication of quality of the beer produced there, together with the drinking habits of the local population.

On that summer evening our party of about fifteen runners, all men, met in the car park just down the road from the brewery, which was situated in a row of terraced houses. The tour was scheduled to take one and a half hours, the first 45 minutes being a tour of the process, held mainly on the ground and the upper two floors. Then we went into the bar, which was situated in the cellar immediately beneath the ground floor. We were allowed to drink as much beer as we could in the 45 minutes remaining. The floor of this cellar was of dark grey cobblestones, the walls were brick-built, the lines of mortar showing clearly under the multiple coats of white emulsion. This enhanced the hygienic appearance, a further contribution being afforded by the low temperature in the cellar. Against three of the walls were wooden trestles, on which were aluminium beer kegs lying on their sides. The kegs were connected to plastic taps by means of clear plastic tubing.

I made my way to one of the kegs marked, appropriately enough, "Fell Runner," a new brew marketed by Hartley's and drank smoothly, the beer "hardly touching the sides of my mouth and gullet". Full marks to Hartley's for the superb texture and taste. However the bar in the brewery must be the pinnacle of quality for any beer, I suppose. For my next pint I went to the "XB", another new brew. Conversation was hushed, then gradually increased in volume as the process of drinking took over. I then tried two more beers, whose names escape me.

All too soon the 45 minutes was up, by which time I had sunk four pints. Then, I started totting up. "I saw Roly, a marathon runner who ran a best time of 2 hours 23 minutes in the London Marathon shortly afterwards. "How many pints, Roly," His eyes were, understandably, shining," Err, eight Barry," he muttered, apologetically. I winced. He had started running just to lose weight but enjoyed the beer and regularly put on weight and took it of by running. "How many pints, Ray?" I shouted across the room to the tall lean figure across the room?" He stopped drinking for a moment, paused, frowned, put the glass down, started counting on his fingers, then smiled and said, "Six, Barry, I think." He ran 10k's. He then put the glass to his lips to empty the glass. The walk back to the cars was unsteady, understandably, but not boisterous. We all then went our own ways, driven by people who had not been drinking. A grand evening was had by all.

## **Beer as a Training Incentive**

Historically, the competition year for club runners was cross country in the winter, track in the summer and relays, both cross country and road in the few weeks between cross country and summer track competitions, in Spring and Autumn. Road relays were either point-to-point, i.e. London to Brighton, Bristol to Weston super-Mare, Chichester to Portsmouth, Manchester to Liverpool, etc, each race being divided into legs from three to six miles, or on a circuit. Point to point relays on the road have been discontinued, because of Health and Safety considerations resulting from increased road traffic and increased costs for policing. The major road relays held now are in closed parks, and culminate in the Area championships and the National Championship usually held in Sutton Park in Sutton Coldfield, for men and women. Entry to the National Championship is by competing in the Area Championship in the (North, South, or Midlands etc.), the criteria for entry going on to the National Championship being stated at the time. Racing in the National in Sutton Park presents a club athlete with an opportunity to race over the same road and distance as all the best runners in the country over many years over that course and these national relays provide a true yardstick of running standards in this country.

In 1996 I was a member of Barrow & Furness Striders AC and coached a number of athletes there. This club was and still is a small club in the Athletics world and had entered the Northern 12 Stage Races for many years without progressing to the National. In an attempt to improve our chances of getting to the National 12 Stage in Sutton Park I realised that we had to get inside the top 20 or so teams in the Northern 12 Stage and hit upon the inducement of offering a pint of beer per man if we qualified to go to the National that year. I inserted the provisos that the beer was to be at Barrow prices and only after we had run in the National. The result was that in that year we went to Sutton Park and finished 35th overall, an excellent performance, considering that teams went to the National from the South, Midlands and the North and our expected position would have been in the high forties or fifties. On the riotous way home on the minibus, we stopped at the Ship Inn at Greenod, fifteen miles away from Barrow. I bought fourteen pints, twelve for the team, one for me and one for stalwart Roly who was injured on the day and who drove the minibus.

Is beer the only inducement to which runners respond? Would we have finished higher up if I had promised the runners two pints each? Possibly not, because a year later we finished 29th in the Northern 12 stage in Leeds and did not make the National that year, or subsequently until 2010, as mentioned in Chapter 4, Athletics Folklore.

END

# CHAPTER 10

# ONLY ONE FOOT WET—THE STEEPLECHASE

## Why "Only One Foot Wet"

In the early 1990's I was the Event Coach for Steeplechase for the British Athletics Federation (B.A.F.) in the Northern Division, which included Cumbria, North Yorkshire, Northumberland and Durham. I conducted coaching sessions in Jarrow throughout the winter, and this involved a drive of 130 miles each way from my home in Barrow-in-Furness, in Cumbria. I started to write a book about the steeplechase and often talked about this project to my drinking friends in my local at that time, The Bay Horse, in Ireleth, Cumbria. Sadly that pub is now just another private house, in a lovely location overlooking the Duddon estuary and sadly also the book did not come to fruition. This was primarily because there was no interest shown by publishers I approached and because I was unable to afford the publishing costs myself. Around the table were the usual group but on this occasion we were joined by Brenda, the wife of Jim, a regular member at our group. On hearing about my writing intentions, she said, "Oh, the steeplechase. Isn't that where they get only one foot wet?" She was a nursing auxiliary in the local hospital and was non-athletic but her comment indicated that she watched the Athletics on TV and the phrase had stuck with her. It seemed such a good title for my intended, but later, non-existent book and also for this chapter.

## Steeplechase History

The steeplechase event has its origins in the world of hunting and the chase, where the necessity to clear formidable obstacles was paramount and horses of great strength and agility were required, together with speed. The origins of horses bred specifically for hunting and the chase go back to Asia Minor before 4000BC. Steeplechase races for horses were a logical development from hunting, which took place all over the British Isles. The first recorded steeplechase race for men on horseback in recent times took place in 1752 in County Cork in Ireland when Mr. Edmund Blake and Mr. O'Callaghan raced over 4.1/2 miles between Buttevant Church and St. Leger Church. The most prominent landmarks in the flat countryside were the church steeples and these became natural markers to the finish points of races. The riders selected their own courses and aimed for that steeple in the distance and these races became known as steeplechases. Steeplechase racing for horses soon spread into other areas of the British Isles and then into France and Spain in 1840 and in the USA in 1844. The major steeplechase race for horses in England is the Grand National, held every spring at Aintree, Liverpool and run for the first time in 1839. This particular race is over 4.1/2 miles and includes 30 jumps.

The first recorded steeplechase for men is said to have taken place on a flat marshy farm at Binsey, two miles north west of Oxford city centre. As the story goes, on the evening after a conventional steeplechase race on horseback, "The College Grind" at Exeter College Oxford in 1850, a number of students met in the rooms of R.F. Bowles for a drink and to discuss the events of the day. They may have been bored with the repetitive nature of their races, it is not known for sure. One of the party, Halifax Wyatt, had been thrown from his horse in the race that day and in some exasperation said, "Sooner than ride that brute again I'd rather run across country on foot."

"Well why not." said his friends.

His suggestion was taken up and a "College Foot Grind" was organised. A committee was formed, officials for the race meeting were appointed and a notice of the meeting posted on a blackboard in the porter's lodge as was usual at the time and entries requested. In accordance with custom a list of side stakes was produced and bets were placed.

The race, over two miles, was held at Binsey in the autumn of that year, the actual date not being known. The ground was reported to be "very wet, some fields swimming in water, the brook banks high with the take off soft". There were 24 starters and they were dressed in cricket flannels and cricket boots and all were "determined to do or die."

The start was fast but ground conditions and levels of fitness of the runners took their toll. Over the last fence Halifax Wyatt gained a few yards over second placed Jas Aitken who just held off J. Scott in third. The time was slow as would be expected because of the wet ground, the large fences and the flannel trousers, which hindered the runners. One can only speculate on the post race celebrations.

During the late 18th and the 19th century professional Athletics meetings known as "Pedestrianism" were held all over the country. Details of forthcoming meetings and the results were reported in "Bells Life" in London and the "Sporting Chronicle" and other regional newspapers. Often more than 50 such meetings were advertised weekly. Races were often over a single distance, often a challenge was thrown out and there was usually prize money to be won (and stakes to be lost). Professional and amateur athletes co-existed at that time.

Following the race at Binsey in 1850 it is believed that steeplechase races were held at various venues throughout the country where the specific events would be decided locally. In Cumbria the Ulverston Advertiser reported, "A one mile steeplechase was held round the Barrow Tower". In Bells Life of London it was reported that on 1 July 1860 a 500-yard handicap steeplechase race was held in London.

An annual steeplechase was first held in 1858 at the Varsity match between Oxford and Cambridge Universities. They continued to be held until 1864 when a 2-mile steeplechase was one of the 8 events on the programme. This race was won by R.G. Garnett (Rugby and Trinity) running for Cambridge. In that particular race it is reported, "the brook jump was swollen by floods". On 9 July that year Bell's Life reported that R.G. Garnett (the same man possibly) was second to his brother G. Garnett in the 1 mile steeplechase held at the Liverpool Olympic Festival. It is further reported that in the Varsity match of 1867 the steeplechase was replaced by a 2-mile race, the reasons not being stated. For many years the steeplechase was looked on as "comic relief where the water jumps were almost impossible to negotiate, the water being deep and the barriers overgrown" (The Badminton Library Of Sports and Pastimes—Athletics and Football).

Steeplechase races were held at the Olympic Games from 1900 onwards. In Paris in 1900 there were two steeplechase races, one at 2500 metres, the other at 4000 metres. Both were "over stone fences, a water jump hurdle and other obstacles." The shorter race was won by the Canadian George Orton in 7m 34.4s with Sidney Robinson of Great Britain second in 7m 38.0s. The longer race was a clean sweep for Great Britain, first being John Rimmer of Liverpool in 12m 58.4s. Second was Charles Bennett in 12m 58.6s with Sidney Robinson third.

In these Paris Games Bennett became Britain's first Olympics gold medallist by doubling or trebling up by winning the 1500 metres in 4m 06s and the 5000 metres in 15m 20s. These times were unofficial world bests and allow a useful comparison with modern day performances despite the fact that they were set on cinder or dirt surfaces and footware and clothing worn by the competitors were probably much heavier than nowadays. In the Olympic Games in St Louis in 1904 the steeplechase (2500 metres) was won by James Lightbody of the USA in 7m 39.6s. In the London Games in 1908 the winner was Arthur Russell of Great Britain in 10m 47.8s and at the next Games, held in Stockholm in 1912, the steeplechase was not held at all.

In 1913 the International Amateur Athletic Federation (I.A.A.F.) decided on a standard distance of 3000 metres for the steeplechase for future Olympic Games. The First World War intervened and the first Olympic Champion over 3000 metres was Percy Hodge of Great Britain who won in Antwerp in 1920 in 10m 0.4s. Between 1920 and 1950 the Scandinavians were the undoubted masters of distance running and dominated the steeplechase. Athletes from Finland took first three places in the Olympic Games of 1924 (Paris) and 1928 (Amsterdam) and that country provided the individual winner in 1932 (Los Angeles) and 1936 (Berlin) with the exciting Volman Iso Hollo. In the years immediately after the war the event-domination changed to Sweden who won gold, silver and bronze medals in London (1948).

In 1954 at its congress in Berne, Switzerland, the I.A.A.F. standardised the rules for the event. In that year the first official world record was set by Hungarian Sandor Rosnyoi when he won the European Championships in

Berne in 8m 49.6s, although at the time the unofficial world best time of 8m 44.4s had been set by Olaui Rinteenpaa of Finland. In Great Britain the A.A.A. had retained their traditional two mile steeplechase until 1954 when the first champion at the new 3000 metre distance was Ken Johnson in a time of 9m 00.8s. The current (2011) British record of 8m 07.96s was set in September 1988 by Mark Rowland in Seoul. However, much of this improvement must be due to improved running track surfaces, improved running shoes and more intensive training.

From 1972 the event has been dominated by yet another country, Kenya, although mention must be made of Anders Garderud (Sweden), who took the title in Montreal in 1976 and Bronislaw Malinovski (Poland), the winner in 1980 (Moscow) in times which compare favourably with the best times recorded since. In the Games of 1976 and 1980 political interference prevented the Kenyan athletes from competing so it is unwise to speculate too deeply on the possible outcome had they been there. However, as has already been said, since 1978 every world record in the event has been set by Kenyans and athletes of that country have won six of the nine medals awarded in the Olympic Games of 1984 (Los Angeles), 1988 (Seoul) and 1992 (Barcelona) and most of the medals since then.

Women started to run the steeplechase in the late 1980's, the distance then being limited to 2000 metres and the majority of athletes were from Eastern Europe. However the main distance for women has become 3000 metres, the main leading performers being under

9 minutes ad from Eastern Europe and, not surprisingly, from Kenya.

In the 1990's I was involved with other steeplechase coaches in the UK in discussions about the recommended dimensions of the barriers for women, the eventual decision being that the height of the barriers for them would be 2 feet 6 inches (76.2cms), rather than the 3 feet (91.4cms), which is the height for men. I disagreed because I felt and demonstrated that women could negotiate the higher barrier successfully. I did this, without consciously thinking about it, when I was coaching schoolchildren (boys and girls) on a school playing field in running and I introduced them to hurdling. For this I used the hurdles used for track sprint hurdles races, which are adjustable in increments of three inches. After they had successfully completed the introductory drills and runs over the hurdles set at lower heights I arranged two hurdles 10 yards apart, one set at 2 feet six inches, one at three feet. The children were waiting in line thirty yards away and I walked towards them and said, "OK, go over whichever one you want." After a slight hesitation the child in pole position ran and flew over one of the hurdles, I don't remember which one. The children into two lines, one ran over the lower hurdle, the other over the higher hurdle. The children hurdled effectively over the two hurdles, as many girls going over the higher hurdle as boys. "Enjoy that did you?" I asked. Many heads nodded and the children went over their preferred hurdle. I was able to stand back and observe their relaxed attitude and hurdling fluency and the flushed excitement in their faces at the end.

There was an interesting sequel to my work with the school children some years or more later when I was shopping in one of the supermarkets in Barrow and had put my purchases onto the conveyor belt at the checkout. The belt moved forward and then stopped. The lady on the checkout put out her hand to scan my first item and as I was looking down at my purchases I noticed that the hand also had stopped. I looked up to find that the lady was staring at me intently me. She paused, smiled and then said, "You taught us to hurdle didn't you?" I forget my reply, but thought that she had enjoyed the experience she had spoken about.

Nowadays the women run the same distances as men, i.e. the race distance for Senior Women is 3000 metres but barrier height is reduced to 2 feet 6 inches.

## The Format

In its present form the steeplechase is run on a 400 metre synthetic track and in each complete lap there are four steeplechase barriers and one water jump. Each of these obstacles is 3 feet (0.91 metres) high for men, 2 feet 6 inches (76.2 cms) high for women and 12 feet (3.96 metres) long and each athlete must go over them. The water jump is normally on the inside of the track but in many major stadia around the world and some in Great Britain the water jump is on the outside.

The position of the water jump on the track modifies the length of each lap run by the athletes and must be taken into consideration by coaches and athletes when calculating training and racing lap times and race tactics. The lap length is about 394 metres with the water jump on the inside of the track and about 420 metres with it on the outside. The actual distances will depend on the individual track and will be defined in the track drawings. All steeplechasers and their coaches must be aware of the different positions of the start for the different distances and also the different water jump positions.

Race distances have been standardised at 3000 metres for senior men and women and are reduced for younger athletes. For the 3000 metres with the water jump on the inside of the track these distances represent 7.6, 5.1 and 3.8 laps and the athletes run seven complete laps with barriers and water jump for the 3000 metres. It is of interest that best times for 1500 metre steeplechase and the mile have always been very close and also the times for 3000 metre steeplechase and the 2 miles. In August 1992 just three days after breaking the world record for the 3000 metre flat in 7m 28.96s Moses Kiptanui of Kenya set a new world record for 3000m steeplechase of 8m 02.08s, a difference of 31.04 Seconds. This gave us a measurement of the time differential between the flat and the same distance over barriers and water jump. This differential is also a measure of the athlete's hurdling abilities and is in my opinion a valuable parameter for use by steeplechase coaches. In that year Kiptanui ranked first in the world in the 5000 metres flat in 13m 00.93 and 12th in the 1500m with 3m 34.00. He was a magnificent runner. Differentials recorded by international standard athletes ranged from 15.78s (Tom Hanlon) to 44.9s (Kip

Keino), so improvement in hurdling technique offers the athlete significant improvement in performance.

The event has moved on beyond all recognition, as have all other events because of the inevitable law which says that what one man or woman has done another can do better and it is almost impossible to compare competitors in different eras, if only because of technological improvements. In the present, in May 2010 the world records for the 3000 metres steeplechases are 7m 53.63s by Saif Saaeed Shaheen, a Kenyan-born citizen of Qatar, set in Brussels in September 2004 and 8m 58.81s set by Guinara Galkina of Russia in August 2008 in Beijing. The corresponding best times for the UK are 8m 07.96 by Mark Rowlands set in Seoul in September 1988 and Helen Clithero's 9m 29.14s set in August 2008 in Beijing. Inevitably all these times will improve.

These times indicate that steeplechasers will be competent middle distance runners, although there is much debate as to whether they ideally come from the 1500 metre region or the 5000 metre region. There are examples of both—see the standards set by Moses Kiptanui in the above paragraph. The view of the author is that the 1500 metre region and training is more appropriate to the steeplechase because of the need for fast leg action over the barriers and the necessity to maintain speed as an essential ingredient in the repertoire of any middle distance runner.

## The Demands of the Steeplechase

In a flat race the runner can often relax and can be carried along by the pace and sit in. This does not happen in the steeplechase because those barriers will not go away. When the runner clears one barrier he must concentrate on the next. Most falls in steeplechasing occur because the athlete gets his timing wrong on the approach and collides with the barrier or water jump, or another athlete. The steeplechase is fatiguing, demanding in the extreme, requires intense concentration, and is exciting because of the ever-present possibility of collision with a barrier. It is also beautiful because of the grace of the hurdling techniques applied, particularly over the water jump. In addition it is satisfying to the athlete because it is so difficult.

Every steeplechaser is a runner but not every runner is a steeplechaser. He/she must above all be a strong runner with high levels of strength-endurance, special strength and speed-endurance (the ability to run fast in an endurance-environment). He/she must have exceptionally high levels of concentration and his mobility and range of movement must be equal to those of the sprint hurdler.

The benefits to any runner in taking to the steeplechase are:

1.  Improved mobility and strength, particularly about the pelvic girdle, which will enable the athlete to run faster over other (flat) race distances.

2. Improved levels of concentration with the same benefits as in 1.
3. More options for the team manager and club as well as for the athlete.

## Requirements of the steeplechaser

The steeplechaser should ideally:

1. be a strong runner.
2. be able to hurdle off either leg with equal facility.
3. adopt a progressive training and racing programme including both flat running and steeplechase elements.

## Training and racing programme

From the coaching viewpoint we use the 400-metre hurdle technique modified to the athlete's body and to the endurance demands of the event. Each athlete has a different body structure and the aim of any steeplechase technique training must be to enable him/her to run over the barriers with minimum expenditure of energy, not necessarily to turn him/her into a sprint hurdler. Technical elements must be taught until the athlete becomes proficient at hurdling and the water jump and then they must be practised at times under fatigue conditions. Good technique lends itself to analysis, fault-correction and improvement, particularly in the reduction of the differential.

To avoid confusion two terms used interchangeably are defined.

1.  Hurdles—are as used in sprint hurdles races and are designed to topple over when struck.
2.  Barriers—are solid wooden or metal constructions placed around the track across three lanes. They do not move and are usually painful when struck by the athlete.

Sprint hurdles are used for teaching hurdle technique and barriers are used for water jump simulation and bulk training sessions.

Every aspect of the steeplechase requires a "running" element and the steeplechaser must learn to "run" over the steeplechase barriers and water jump. The first steps of this process are best performed with sprint hurdles on a track as described below and safety and injury prevention must be uppermost in the minds of coaches and athletes. Because of repetitive landings off either foot and the requirement for high levels of pelvic girdle mobility, sessions must be limited to what the athlete can take without injury.

## **Water Jump**

Poor technique over the water jump results in more energy and time loss than anything else and much attention should be paid to it. I recommend that the same lead leg should be used because of the complex movements required. Only one foot should get wet. I advise athletes against clearing the water jump and water completely because of excessive use of energy and safety. The water helps to cushion the shock of landing. The aim should be to run onto the rail of the barrier, keep low, run off it, land and run out of the water, all in one continuous running sequence.

## Technique—Why bother

Some years ago a documentary was shown on BBC TV showing a Kenyan village where large groups of runners, mainly male, ages from 10 upwards, raced round a circuit containing fences made from brushwood. In such an intensely competitive environment it is not surprising that they become such good runners and of course steeplechasers. They make space for hurdles naturally, although with a hurdling technique which leaves much to be desired from a classical hurdling point of view. The better an athlete can run over barriers the faster times he will set, hence the justification in my mind for teaching such technique. I accept that many athletes have performed well while excluding hurdles or mobility training, but I argue that they would they have been faster by including it.

END

# CHAPTER 11

# THE RUNNER AND DOGS

The British are passionately fond of their dogs and are prepared to defend them vehemently if necessary should the occasion present itself. The dog itself is never (in the eyes of the owner) at fault, even if they exhibit violent and sometimes dangerous behaviour. "Oh, he's never done that before. He's always been so well behaved." is a comment I have heard more than once. To be fair, many dogs are placid, well-behaved creatures, as are their owners when you see them on the street. Often the dog is connected to the owner with a retractable, extendable lead, which can stretch right across a pavement and across the road as well. If not correctly deployed this line can be a hazard for the unwary runner as a tripping device.

To give another picture of the dog, years ago there used to be an afternoon of road races at Eastleigh, just north of Southampton. The Senior Men ran five miles, the younger athletes running shorter distances. Memory does not confirm whether there was a women's race. With every race, at the start the runners were joined by a white collie type dog, which ran with the leaders, never interfering with the runners. After the first race that dog went off with the leaders in each of the races. He must have been a fit dog. Or maybe he just liked the company.

In rural Massachusetts in 1970 I had my experiences of the American dog. In most cases the breed was the German Shepherd (Alsatian). Half of the dogs were tied up; the other half should have been. All were half-wild. So when I ran past their territory, I got to know the doggy welcomes, insults and vulgarities I was likely to receive. The methods of attaching the dog to its garden or kennel, or house were varied. Some dogs were permanently tethered, imprisonment starting with a chain twenty feet or so long attached to its collar. Sometimes the other end of the chain was attached to a stake, a kennel, a tree or the house. But occasionally the other end was attached via a metal ring to another length of chain or line, which hung permanently about ten feet above ground level and can be fifty yards in length. This enabled the dog to achieve high and frightening speeds as it raced towards me when I was passing. The result in these latter cases was always the same. The dog always seemed delighted to see me, barked furiously and rushed towards me to the limit of its chain. Where tethered to the line above the ground, the dog increased speed and barking frenzy until its forward motion was brought to a halt by the tightening of its chain on the line. The dog left the ground and swung about the horizontal axis, backward and forwards, showing its stomach and paws to me. It then swung back. The barking changed into a choking sound (not surprisingly), the dog swung, its legs reaching down to the ground and the barking began afresh. Each time I saw this happen I winced at the thought of what would happen should the chain break and the dog would continue its journey at high speed in my direction.

Later, back in England, I encountered another group of canines, those who are allowed to go free despite being only half-wild, or half-trained. This presented another potential cause for concern to the runner. A few, wiser, doggy beings would look upon my passing with a sniff, yawn or disdain, but the majority often had predictably violent intentions. They would rush out from their spot on the lawn and race towards me, barking furiously, running very fast while they are on their territory, safe behind their own front gates and hedges. Presumably they were anxious to alert their owners to a probable hostile presence. If their gate was open for them to rush through, they did just that, but then they slowed down when outside their territorial limit. If one decided to attack me it would invariably circle to attack from the rear, then make a move to whichever foot or lower leg was nearest to them. Their aggression and barking usually reduced when I continued to run away from their territory. To help this process I would continue to run past the dog, but turn so as always to face the dog, even if it meant that I could be running backwards for a short distance.

For that more resolute minority of dogs, some trained to kill, who pressed home the attack, they would swing in to my leg, jaws open with the intent to bite, my remedy was simply to launch a kick at the underside of the jaw. If timed to perfection this manoeuvre has a most salutary effect on the dog, which will probably not attack a runner again. While I have adopted a light-hearted approach to this potentially lethal behaviour on the part of the dog I must mention that if the dog makes a habit of attacking anyone running, it can also attack a child, with probably catastrophic effects. I had harsh words with one dog owner about this one day in Northern England much later, but he did not seem to be concerned about any child being savaged by his dog.

It should be mentioned that if the defensive mechanism mentioned above is not timed to perfection the result can be anything from a failure to connect at all by the dog to a torn trouser and a bleeding leg for the runner. Even if the runner stops or walks the dog's intentions must be carefully monitored. On those rare occasions when the dog does not conform to the norm each case must be treated on its merits. Where a dog is small, it can hopefully be treated as shown above. But when it is big or there are two of them then the run becomes a walk, a defensive posture being adopted. The three main lines of defense (defence) are:

1.  A backward walk to get out of the danger zone.
2.  A constant stare at the dog(s)—no dog likes to attack from the front.
3.  Make yourself as large as possible. Hands should be raised in a defensive boxing stance but with the arms raised high and apart, with the edges of the hands ready to chop downwards onto the dog's head like an executioner's axe.

4.  Make as much noise as possible, to scare the dog.

The final ultimate weapon must be the willingness to make the dog pay should he sink tooth into flesh. Only once has this happened to me when I was attacked by two large German Shepherds (Alsations), one from either side. I stopped and backed against a tree—then a wild kick drove the dogs back a pace. I spied a large stone at my feet and I picked it up. Immediately the dogs turned and ran, pursued by the stone, which fell behind them. My action of bending to pick up the stone, or imaginary stone, could have been enough to send them into a retreat.

On one occasion a large Alsatian preferred to run after and bark at cars rather than at me. He must have been perverted.

END

# CHAPTER 12

# COACHING RUNNING FOR ATHLETICS AND OTHER SPORTS

## Contents List

Each of these elements is now discussed.

## 1. Introduction to Coaching

This chapter enables me to give to the reader a glimpse of the world of an Athletics Club running coach. The views expressed are mine and I am aware that there will be strong disagreement among coaches and athletes with what I say. Throughout my life I have found this to be the case, whatever the subject and believe that instant disagreement is a human characteristic. This chapter is not intended as a definitive manual for coaches or athletes and I recognise that there will always be different approaches to achieving any goal.

The world of Athletics and indeed of all sports has become the preserve of the sports scientists who have defined and measured very accurately most body functions and parameters and who try to codify and provide theorems for improved performance. I had difficulty with the scientific theories and based my coaching on the literature prevailing at the time and modified this when faced with the practical problem of coaxing athletes to push themselves to their limits. In circumstances where I could not follow a planned and proper course I worked out practical solutions, some of which worked, some did not. In this way I built up a repertoire of primarily running-specific sessions which worked well for the athletes and have used this approach throughout my coaching career.

## 2. Definition—Coaching

The published profiles of most elite athletes usually include a specific named coach but in an athlete's career he comes under the influence of other coaches and talks to other athletes. It is correct in my view for him to raise questions with his coach and for the coach to answer them. The coach can control sessions on a track but must be prepared to take a back seat when the athlete takes part in squad sessions with other athletes of his own standard. In these sessions the athlete experiences and must learn to deal with race-type intensities and the accompanying physical and psychological sensations.

The coach strives to improve the performance of any athlete he works with and can only do this in the period in which the athlete is following his direction. I have heard it said that the worth of the coach can be assessed by the number of international standard athletes he has in his charge. In my view the coach has one main parameter under which he can be judged, namely has the athlete improved while with the coach. The coach utilises the "What" and the "How" of coaching. The "What" refers to the actual sessions, exercises, routines which the athlete performs, such as the training sessions, distances, recovery period, type of surface, intensity, i.e. times expected from the athlete for a particular event. These can be taught on courses or read about in articles or books. The "How" relates to the way in which these are put together for a particular athlete and this cannot be taught, but comes from the experience of the coach, sometimes intuitively, sometimes logically. What works for one athlete may not work for another. The best coaches manage to select the correct path for the athlete. It is not easy.

This chapter is written as though for a male athlete, but applies equally to female athletes. Coaching one-to-one is the finest example of man-management available. The successful coach must motivate the athlete, devise a plan for his successful future, implement the plan to improve performance levels, taking the athlete into areas in which injury is never far away and he must work on the athlete's body and mind. To do this the coach must ideally be knowledgeable in anatomy, physiology, psychology, and of course practical knowledge of the event being coached. He must also plan a course of training for the athlete for implementation either individually or in a group. Further requirements are the ability to survive and operate in weather conditions from arctic winds to tropical heat, heavy rain and to conduct a session with up to a dozen athletes. A useful and essential ingredient for success is a powerful voice capable of penetrating, at a distance of 50 metres, that pain-relieving cocoon in which an athlete surrounds himself in the latter stages of a race or training session.

Most Athletics clubs have over the years an individual or individuals who have coached the younger members, based on a desire to put something back into their sport. Often these coaches were non-qualified, wanted to help the younger generation, sometimes with the hope in their mind that the next lad or lass who came into the club would be their passport to coaching greatness and recognition. Each coach attracted athletes to his group because he was always there and had served the club loyally and well. The older generations live their dreams through the performances of the young and most clubs have older athletes who have given their time and experience to coaching, their coaching being based on their own experiences. From these ranks of unqualified coaches have come some superb coaches, many of whom have guided athletes to the highest levels at National, Olympic and World Championships, often with a blend of their own competitive experiences with common sense and years of experience as competitive athletes.

Each coach has his own personality and many have become protective of "their" athletes. In some clubs there has been friction between some coaches and also the athletes of each group. At times, because of these underlying frictions within a club, movement of an athlete from one coach to another or from one club to another, has sometimes been accompanied by adverse comment and actions. The best service a coach can provide to youngsters is to teach them to love to run for its own sake, just to enjoy the feeling of running freely. However some runners prefer to do their own thing and I can understand this approach, having done that myself.

The situation described above is not satisfactory because there is no standard set of instructions or syllabus for coaching runners, despite many attempts by Athletics authorities to provide such a system. Maybe it is impossible, because the most valued coaching asset is the ability to decide on the right session and this becomes better with experience. In profiles of elite athletes shown in Athletics publications the one common element is that each of them does enormous amounts of training on their own, just to stay at a certain level. Most competitive international-standard runners spend three hours or more per day training, for many years, to include time for training sessions and then showering, before returning to his/her family work and other activities. The key to success is for the athlete to perform just the right session to stretch the appropriate body muscle and mental systems and this decision is the difficult bit. Where the athlete is responsible for his own decisions, his main difficulty is to decide on the right session for continued improvement.

A description of my own approach to becoming qualified as a running coach may help to explain my opinion. Like most athletes I was in full time employment, my training and competitions being done in my spare time. In the 1960's I was a member of Reading Athletic Club, my career bests being 2m 07.4s half mile, 4m 37.4s mile, 15m 40s three miles, 32m 30s six miles, all on cinder tracks, and ten miles on the road in 57m 02 seconds. My main love was cross-country, my best results being 151st in the Inter-Counties Championships in 1961, running for Berkshire and 340th in the National Cross Country Champs in the same year when I was 27. These positions may seem to a non-Athletics person to be unremarkable but the standards in the 1960's were high. In 1974, then aged 39 I ran my best marathon time of 2h 52m 59s in the Harlow Marathon.

From my coaching records I have listed 139 athletes who featured in my sessions from 1980 to 2004. This list excludes all Elite athletes in Northern squad sessions and also those I coached professionally as a Fitness

Consultant. Some stayed for just one session, some stayed for years. Most became friends. In addition to those named I show statements like "12 athletes doing hill session." I have had the good fortune to work as a coach with many fine people, mostly club-level athletes, some reaching higher levels. I have worked with numbers of athletes, male and female, young and old over events from 800 metres to the marathon, including the steeplechase. As a coach my major specialities were 800 metres and steeplechase, but in a club environment a coach attracts other athletes, some of whom look first of all at what other coaches or athletes are doing and then decide who they would like to join. At any one venue on club training night there may be three or four groups of runners under different coaches, doing different things. My groups attracted additional athletes, male and female, of different capabilities and training nights tended to be intense occasions.

In the late 1970's, when it was obvious to me and to others that my times on the track were slowing, I started chatting to Peter, a 20-year-old policeman who ran 800 metres for the club and we agreed that I would coach him. He looked me straight in the eye and said, "OK, what do I do now?" I took a deep breath, thought quickly and set him a standard session, which, along with many athletes, I had done many times. This was probably something like 8 x 400 metres on the track with 200-metre jog recovery. We agreed to meet again and that night I started to read everything I could find on coaching runners. I realised that if I was to be of any use to him as a coach I must always be just one step ahead of him with every session, just to maintain his improvement. Shortly afterwards I enrolled on a coaching course organised by the Amateur Athletic Association (A.A.A.) and moved up the coaching ladder to Senior Coach 800/1500 and 5,000/10,000 metres. I have been learning ever since, much of it from the athletes I have worked with. A few years later, for a period of three years, Peter became British Police 800 metre and 1500 metre champion and best 800 and 1500 metre times of 1min 52.2secs and 3min 54.0 secs. We must have done something right because he agreed to write the foreword to this book.

My training group gradually grew as other athletes joined. Later, an athlete who specialised in the steeplechase, joined and I had to repeat my exercise on reading as much as I could about this event, just to keep ahead of him. For this event I had to include reading about the hurdles events, particularly the 400 metre hurdles. From that time I worked with flat runners and steeplechasers and encouraged other athletes to take up this demanding event. Later I added the Steeplechase to my Senior Coach qualification. I have continued to coach, and have continued to learn, from athletics publications and also from the athletes.

In 1994, following the change in management of Athletics in the UK to The British Athletics Federation (B.A.F.) my coaching qualification became a Level 4 Coach, (Endurance), a term which encompassed all the running events from 800 metres to ultra marathons. From 1988 until 2000 I was the Event Coach for steeplechase for Northern Division, B.A.A.B (and later

B.A.F.) and conducted regular Elite Squad sessions. In addition to coaching athletes I prepared and delivered courses for Coach Education within the Northern Division.

## 3. Definition-Runner

The word "Runner" means anyone who runs, in an individual sport such as Athletics, or in a team sport such as rugby, football, hockey, or just for general fitness. It has always been a fundamental human activity, if only initially to flee from wild animals or human enemies. It was probably one of the first competitive elements in all societies among children while they were growing up, in order to find out "Who is the fastest of us all?" Running is a necessary ingredient in many sports, such as football, rugby, hockey, cricket, and can be used for general cardio-vascular improvement. Generally sportsmen in these other sports dislike running, probably because it can be soul-destroying and boring. They would much rather use their time with the ball, kicking, catching, running with it, etc.

In most team sports, running occupies a subsidiary role in the various skill elements required by the sport's practitioner, all of which must be used in performing the event well. For three years after being made redundant in Cumbria I worked as a Fitness Consultant with football and rugby players and athletes from running clubs. From watching football and rugby matches on TV and sports fields I tried to analyse energy level expenditure patterns in their sports and prepared sessions incorporating what I thought were necessary elements to improve their running and ultimately their playing performance. My fundamental objective was to improve their cardio-vascular efficiency, i.e. their ability to transport sufficient oxygen to their muscles and brains and to remove waste products from the muscles. If the cardio-vascular system cannot deliver oxygen in the blood adequately for the task being performed, fatigue sets in with accompanying loss of speed of movement, speed of thought, movement accuracy, etc. The players and some coaches were initially hostile when I conducted fitness sessions but their attitudes changed when their playing standards improved.

I devised running-based fitness training sessions for the players and on more than one occasion the session ended with a round of applause from the players. They were essentially very competitive individuals and were used to driving themselves hard when doing what they wanted to do. Each session, of about ninety minutes' duration, was composed of a variety of elements, starting with running (the boring bit) as an introductory necessity of short duration, just to improve blood flow and to prepare them for the more technical speed and power elements. This warm up run and stretching routine was followed by series of drills, sprints and power exercises, some of which were competitive. Usually the players detested the introductory run but enjoyed the later competitive elements. The ability to run faster than the opposition without the ball gives a player time to think and act quicker than the opposition.

# 4. The Practical Coaching Environment

## 4.1 The starting Point

A fundamental of all coaching is that every athlete/ player is an individual and must be treated as such. My practice has been to treat every athlete in the same way, regardless of age, sex or standard as follows:

1. Establish the athlete's starting point. i.e. present fitness level.
2. Establish the athlete's preferred event(s) and immediate competition goals.
3. Prepare an improvement programme specifically for that athlete, to include areas in which improvement in overall running speed can be obtained. This programme must avoid injury, eliminate boredom, that destroyer of so much well-meant efforts, and must be focused on improvement for the athlete.
4. Implement the programme and monitor the results.

In this chapter the word "athlete" means athlete or player and action as recommended above should be applied to each athlete individually. While this statement is glib, obvious and almost condescending it is true and the devil is in the detail, particularly regarding the improvement programme and this matter will now be discussed. The coach can help any athlete who does not know instinctively what is the right session for him to do to ensure that he continues to improve. In practice this becomes difficult because of the infinite variety of sessions, distances, required running speeds, recoveries, running surfaces, together with running environments and this expertise usually does not reside within the athlete's experience. On the occasions where the athlete has this knowledge my advice is for him to do it himself, because then he owes nothing to anybody for his improvement. Runners are intensely competitive individuals and often resent having someone telling them how to run, what to do.

It has already been stated that a prime function of the coach is to help the athlete to improve performance and now I propose to discuss how this can be done.

To run faster we use the "Overload Principle" which states that for a muscle system to become stronger it must be stretched, but not damaged. When the new strength level has been achieved it can then be used as a new baseline from which further improvement (stretch) can be obtained. Before the next stretch can take place the muscle must be allowed to absorb the extension and to operate at the new level. The main difficulty is that it is almost impossible for an athlete performing these exercises, or a coach to know when the limit has been reached and when to stop. This is especially the case when the athlete is highly motivated and desperately wants to complete a set quantity of exercises or runs. This competitive instinct is constant across much human physical activity, i.e. sport, dance, climbing, horsemanship, etc.

The decision as to what the athlete should do for the next session must be a guess at best and my general method is to err on the side of caution, to minimise the possibility of injury.

The coach must prepare the athlete for competition and all its variations and eventualities. The start of a race may be very fast or very slow and the finish may be long and sustained. The athlete should have a race plan or plans for these eventualities. The preparation must consider the athlete's strengths and weaknesses and of course knowing how to incorporate them into the race.

## 4.2 Injury prevention

We start to run when we want to move over the ground faster than walking and just make the legs go faster by increasing both stride length and leg speed. On every stride we push into the ground with a force equal to between two and to five times our body weight, dependent on running speed. The ground does not move so this force is transmitted back up the skeletal structure through each of the major joint complexes, feet, ankles, knees, pelvic girdle, spine and shoulder girdle. It is essential that each joint complex can transmit the forces involved efficiently and without damage. With increased speed, forces within the body increase and injuries can occur in muscles, tissue, blood vessels, etc, and usually result in pain, reduction or cessation of training and unhappiness for the athlete. Within professional and amateur sport injuries occur regularly and most are caused by inadequate preparation or practice. Injury prevention should be high on the coach's agenda in setting sessions. It must be said though that on occasions an injury can occur just by tissue wastage.

A way to reduce the onset of injuries is for the athlete to perform stretching and range of movement exercises appropriate to his event and to him/herself. These exercises, covering mobility and range-of-movement for each joint complex in the body, should be taught early in the athlete's career. Most of us have imperfections somewhere in our bodies and usually these exercises must be continued throughout the athlete's career.

### 4.3 The Five S's

The runner's training programme is based on the Five S's, namely Speed, Strength, Stamina, Suppleness and Skill. Most of a runner's training consists of just going out for a run, from five to twenty miles. Steady running improves only one of the Five 'S's, namely Stamina. However there is little agreement among coaches on the best ways to use these sessions to maximise improvement in running speed. An experienced coach can suggest a balanced route through the many options for an athlete to perform in a session. With regard to the Five S's there are two other S's, which should be mentioned, namely Sex and Stupidity but these are the preserve of the individual athlete. The coach is not normally expected to advise or legislate on either. But see Chapter 9, "Beer Sex and Running".

## 4.4 Running in Heat

At the time of writing, October 2011, there is much discussion about the possibility of the 2022 Football World Cup being held in Qatar, in August. Many western commentators are horrified at this and express concern about the effects of playing football in such high temperatures, despite the proposed provision of air-conditioned stadia for the tournament. My view is that the coaches will be aware of the climatic conditions expected and should be able to prepare the players appropriately. In team sports and sometimes in major Athletics Championships commentators and sometimes coaches make excuses for athletes or players in hot conditions but such excuses are, in my opinion, not acceptable. Most athletics championships and many team sports games are played in summer in major stadia, often in major cities in high temperatures, high humidity and industrial and vehicular pollution. It is the responsibility of the coach to establish—if necessary from published data—the probable environmental conditions in the stadium and to prepare the athletes or players to compete effectively in those conditions, at the expected required intensity for the duration of the race or game. It is of interest that some Caucasian athletes perform very well in high temperature, one example from the endurance running region is Liz McColgan's winning the 10k World Championship in Tokyo in August 1991 in very hot and humid conditions. Another example is Bill Adcocks's winning the Athens Marathon in April 1969, admittedly not the hottest time of year there, wearing plimsolls, in 2hrs 11mins 07secs.

His time on that course has only recently been beaten, by a Kenyan runner.

The most precious ingredient to any runner in his armoury is "Speed", i.e. the ability to do something fast. It may be a leg or arm movement, but also applies to speed of thought and reduced response time to any sudden demands in a race. Many runners believe that they cannot sprint or run fast and accept their lot as slow steady runners. Sadly, if they train regularly at a slow steady pace they will race at a slow steady pace. It is worth considering that fast runners win fast races and fast runners win slow races. However if the runners obtain enjoyment from running slowly, possibly because of social acceptance, camaraderie, feeling of physical well-being, inner pleasure of contributing to charitable cause, etc I respect their choice and say "good luck" to them. But I believe that most runners want to improve their times because that is the source of most enjoyment.

In Barrow-in-Furness, the local all weather running track on Walney Island on the eastern shore of the Irish Sea was run down and not fit for training purposes. So as to maintain training momentum I devised training sessions using road circuits because the track became unusable. I would wait until the last moment before deciding on the specific content of the sessions because I would not know who would be there and more importantly what weather conditions would be like. However I would have thought out a variety of session sequences. The athletes knew that the session would be demanding in the extreme. I would drive down a long road on an industrial estate to our meeting point at a road junction between two garages. As I approached this junction I would see, sometimes through mist or rain, up to twelve athletes, jogging or standing nervously for my arrival and the session to start. The weather there was variable, sometimes misty rain, sometimes gale force winds, although sometimes clear, still and calm. As I drove towards them I could sense their apprehension about the session, which they knew only too well, would be limit-probing and demanding. To my questions, "How are you Ray?" "How are you Pat?", "OK, Sue?" they would look nervously down at the ground or over my shoulder and their responses would be muffled and sometimes inarticulate. They would be scared about the sessions they were about to perform. Although there may be twelve or so athletes there they may need different sessions, different events and different positions in their individual programmes and also of course hostile weather conditions at the training venue. Usually there were no complaints and they were all relieved to get the session under way. The two golden rules always applied were:

1. The session would probe their strengths to the limit.
2. There would be no time allowances for the wind.

At the end of the session, some athletes were unable to stand up immediately, but all were on their feet after a short period and they eventually all gathered round me for the analysis of the session. Usually the results were received positively, usually with a sense of relief that the session was over. Then after a heartfelt "Thank you, Barry," from the individual athletes, the session ended. I looked upon each session as an opportunity for each of us to be together away from the turmoil of our individual busy lives before going back into it, i.e. another successful session completed.

## 5. Coaching—Art or Science?

Is coaching an art or a science? It is both, because the coach must select the correct session to improve another person's performance and then convince the athlete that it is right for him/her at that point in time. This session will be determined firstly from the science, but then modified to cater for the athlete's mental and physical state, weather conditions and possibly by local conditions, such as a bomb scare in a building on the intended course to be used for the session (this actually happened). Most coaches in Athletics and in many sports are essentially amateurs, although very knowledgeable about their sport. Their coaching is their hobby and often serious passion and they do it in addition to their normal job. However coaching, like business or industrial management, is the art of getting results through people and at its best utilises the best man-management practices. The coach/athlete relationship is a team effort in which each contributes, the end product being improvement in performance and enjoyment for the athlete and satisfaction and enjoyment for the coach. Runners are usually highly-motivated athletes, understandably self-centred and selfish as far as their own performance is concerned. They will do what is asked of them provided they believe it is right for them. The athlete must feel that the session will benefit him/her directly and therefore I have tried to have a one-to-one relationship with each. This works well with one athlete but becomes more difficult as numbers increase and virtually impossible with larger numbers (at one time, when working as a Fitness Consultant I worked with groups of over 70 children).

Like all coaches I brought into coaching skills learned in my job. Of particular importance were my man-management skills as a manager in Engineering. I trained as an electronics engineer, studied at night school and became a Chartered Electronics Engineer and also an Associate Certified Accountant. The hours of study and practice in engineering and accountancy left me with an interest in and a facility with numbers and the application of numbers to coaching and athletic performance. This was ideal for Athletics, which is measured by precise numbers, times, distances, etc. With digital stop watches readily available I asked the athletes to take their own times which they relayed to me during the session and I would transpose the data into books at home later that day. This method is adequate for each athlete because his systematic errors would be constant, but it was not good enough to compare performances of different athletes because of their different individual skills at timekeeping. I joked with them that some of them had "sympathetic" or "generous" watches. I have kept detailed records of most coaching sessions I have conducted.

## 6. Coaching Men and Women—Any Difference?

In the 1980's most athletes in my groups were men. I was approached by a lady 800 metre runner who contacted me because of the success of one of my athletes known to her husband, also an athlete. I treated her just like a man 800 metre runner and sent her a similar schedule or programme which I was already using. We met in a local pub for a chat and within the ensuing discussion I looked at her and said something like, "I am not a sympathetic person," a statement which I would have made to a man without hesitation. I happened to be looking into her eyes as I said it and she flinched. Possibly her flinching suggested that she really wanted a sympathetic coach. She attempted to follow my ideas, which I sent by mail, but, not surprisingly, it didn't work and she went her own way. Maybe it was not the right thing to say, but it was my way. Subsequently I preferred to see athletes actually running and performing running routines or exercises which told me much about the athletc's capabilities and think that generally words on paper can be sterile and the coach's personal touch is beneficial.

Later, Fiona (aged 22) accompanied her husband to the sessions and did the same sessions as the men. Over the next three years I recorded her times and she gradually improved to a respectable standard for 3000 metres until she and her husband separated. Years later, Amanda, aged 29, joined my group of her own volition and immediately found that my sessions worked for her. She ran 3 hours 07m in the London Marathon and was second lady in the London to Brighton ultra road race (56 miles). She encouraged other ladies to come along to my sessions and, once again, I treated women athletes no differently to men. I learned from that period that women were more tenacious than the men in performing whatever session I asked them to do. They trusted me and would understand the details of the session quicker than the men and would always finish that session. To me, men and women are all athletes and should expect to work themselves to their individual limits and the coach should treat each with respect and courtesy. My experience suggests that the athletes don't want me to be sympathetic; they want me to be right for them.

With all athletes (and of course coaches) the extremes of exhilaration and despair co-exist. Exhilaration comes when the athlete does well, despair when he/she does badly. An athlete's life contains more kicks than rewards and when the athlete suffers the kicks so does the coach. The coach must be there to help the athlete pick him/herself up and get back into it. In any one season the athlete has no more than three races when everything goes well, when it is so easy and it is those occasions which make the whole season worthwhile. So demanding are the expectations of most athletes that something goes wrong most of the time. In its worst application the athlete doesn't recover and leaves the sport. But the world goes on. In athletics terms any coach/athlete relationship has a natural ending when individual priorities change or when the athlete needs a new stimulus.

At the end of every season I review the season with each of my athletes and then consider the objectives for the next season. I advise any athlete to set targets, short and long term and then try to achieve them. A tangible target provides a focus of mental and physical activity for that part of an athlete's life away from other activities such as work, family, school, emotional problems, etc. Any target should be realistic and based on past achievement and the athlete's abilities.

## 7. The Way to The Top

Often the first step to setting a target is in dreamland; the athlete imagines the packed stadium willing him/her on towards that gold medal. To help any dreamer to go down that road he/she should find out if he/she has the main ingredients for any potential world champion in any sporting or artistic discipline, i.e. talent, life-style to allow the training, availability of coaching and most important, ambition. The fundamental qualities required by any sportsman wishing to reach the highest levels in sport are discussed below:

### 7.1 Talent

Each of us comes into the world with talent for many things, running, sprinting, dancing, mathematics, music, etc. I see daily evidence of superb talent for running among youngsters in play. The problem is being able to develop that talent.

Physiologists point to the presence of fast fibres in muscles, which enable the athlete to respond quickly to a demand for a fast limb movement. In addition genetic or environmental factors are suggested as being vital. There is detectable an inferiority complex among Western athletes about the superiority of African distance runners and the Caribbean sprinters. I disagree with these assumptions and point out that before this can be accepted as fact someone must explain the very high performances set by Caucasian athletes in sprints and endurance events over the years which even now rank highly in the All Time Best tables.

## 7.2 Life-style

Is the athlete's life compatible with allowing him the time to train for his chosen sport? Is he prepared to modify his life style to incorporate the necessary training?

## 7.3 Coaching

Has the athlete access to coaching of the right calibre to move him quickly and correctly from one level to the next? Access to the highest performance levels occurs when the coach is always one step ahead of the athlete and can select the correct programme steps to ensure improvement. More often than not this is not available in the athlete's local environment and he then must go out and find the coach.

## 7.4 Ambition

This is the most important of all. Does he desperately want to succeed in his sport? The future World Champion has an intensity which shrugs off setbacks, which makes him burn inside when defeated and enables him to come back with a firm resolve to improve next time.

## 7.5 Examples

Often some of these ingredients co-exist in one athlete but rarely all. I show below examples of people having different combinations of these qualities, the first one being from outside athletics:

One of my school friends was a skilful, superbly talented inside forward, but spent most of his school life in conflict with the teaching staff because he just did not want to play for the school; he was happy playing village football. High on talent, low on ambition.

In the mid 80's I coached a talented steeplechaser, who worked in Marketing, often on his nerves, often for very long hours and in a high-pressure environment, a combination which prevented him doing the necessary high-intensity training. High on talent, short on life style.

I had dreams in the early 60's of achieving international standard, but with a 4m 38s best mile time this was not to be. High on ambition, low on talent.

In the late 70's I was treated by an osteopath who had seen Steve Ovett training in 1972 at the age of 16 who commented that Ovett was "pathologically intense" about his training and always wanted to train with and beat the men. High on talent, life style and coaching (the great Harry Wilson), but most importantly, high on ambition.

## 8. Setting Targets

In the harsh world of industry I have often heard it said "If the target was achieved it was not hard enough." Most runners can relate to this philosophy and there is some justification in applying demanding targets to runners because of their results-oriented mental approach. A target should be just achievable if the athlete is absolutely at his best. Of all the athletes I have worked with as a coach only one has bettered the target, which he and I agreed at the beginning of his season. In 1991 Peter Willacy ran 9m 27.6s for 3k steeplechase as opposed to the target set of 9m 30s, (he ran 9m 54.0s steeplechase in 1990). For other athletes I had seen things in training, which I was not able to bring out in racing and the season's target was not met, although many personal bests (pb's) were achieved.

Some years ago, following publication of an article of mine, I received a telephone call from a veteran runner about ways he could improve. He was then 44 years of age and had been successful in veteran's races in Yorkshire primarily and had represented Scotland as a veteran. He had no trouble doing his training, which he set himself, but felt the need for a new training plan which would move his running into a higher gear. His main targets for the next year were to break the world record for the Over 45 age group 5k track at the British Veterans Track Championships and to do well in the

World Vets 10k and 25k road Championships to be held in August that year. He ran 70 miles per week regularly and was 45 on July 11. He sent me details of his previous six months training and racing and I sent him programmes by mail, in batches of 12 weeks. In each week he would perform a bulk, short recovery session and also another session composed of distances below 400 metres, once again bulk, short recovery.

On the Road he won the 25k title in 85 minutes 11 seconds, a fast time even for a much younger man. An additional bonus was his 6th place in the 10k in 31 minutes 29 seconds. In addition in the British Vets 10 mile road champs in August that year he was 2nd in 53m 09s, (1st O45), missing the O45 record by seconds. Although one target, of breaking the 5k track world record, had not been achieved; he was satisfied with the overall results. These results demonstrate that training for one distance can produce significant improvements over a range of distances.

Now for two non-running examples of target-setting for myself. In August 2002 my wife and I went to Dubai in August just after the birth of our twin grandsons. I knew that temperatures there were higher than any I had ever experienced and trained hard throughout that year because I knew that the fitter I was the better I could stand the heat. When there I was the "Englishman without his mad dog" and walked every day in the midday sun, in temperatures of 44 °C increasing my time every day and even jogged for 150 metres. The locals raised their eyebrows and I was told curtly by an

American to "Get inside out of the sun." At no time did I experience discomfort in my walks, which I enjoyed.

In 2003 I set another six month target for myself when I had to go into hospital for a prostate operation and I argued that the fitter I could make myself, the better I would heal after the operation. It worked well and on the fourth day after the operation I was sent home. I devised my rehabilitation programme, which started with me staying in the house for a further three days, followed by a short walk per day to build up of physical activity. Sixteen days after the operation I went for a 20 minute jog on soggy grassland close to my house, to raise a sweat and to initiate active recovery. My immediate target then was to get back to where I was just before the operation and this was achieved within the next three months.

## 9. Motivating Young Athletes—To Love to Run

The greatest service a coach can provide to a youngster is get them to love to run. He must inspire and motivate the younger athletes and they will respond well to enthusiasm from the coach. They will willingly do what the coach suggests provided that they get something out of it. This may of course be to enjoy the social world of training or to get closer to someone they fancy and would like to know better.

Youngsters will not take up Athletics because of past heroes. They learn about the greats when they themselves run and want to learn more. Between the ages of 14 and 17 Steve Ovett improved his 800 metre time by 12.7 seconds from 2m 00s to 1m 47.3s. Between the same ages one of my athletes improved by 13.1 seconds, from 2m 03.4s to 1m 50.3s. He was well into his second year with me before his hunger for information about the 800 metre greats became evident. Ovett carried on his career with Harry Wilson as his coach and produced performances the world still marvels at. The young athlete with me went to university and I moved south to Horsham in February 2005 and our athlete-coach team relationship ended. He ran sub 1m 49s in 2005, but improved significantly afterwards. I believe that the 14 to 17 age range for men is the most critical period for development towards senior level. In this age range development should be towards technical and skill areas rather than towards power and endurance.

In wanting to improve, each athlete is selfish and must be provided with a specific programme to allow this improvement. Ideally the coach should measure present performance and ability and then select the appropriate session from an extensive repertoire to take the athlete further down that improvement road. I have managed to achieve this over the last fifteen years, the latest being two male forty somethings, one of whom beat people he had never beaten before in a cross country race in January 2009. Despite the need for specific programmes it is often possible and desirable to devise sessions which can accommodate numbers of athletes present at the session venue.

## **10. The Coach-Athlete Relationship**

In practice I involve each athlete fully by trying to ensure that each understands his/her specific session. The athlete takes his own times, which he shouts to me after every run. After the session I present to each athlete a brief analysis of the results, with comparisons to previous results where possible. A session with a number of athletes becomes a series of multiple athlete/coach teams within a group environment. Usually the group consists of athletes having different event-orientation and varying abilities and fitness levels and it is difficult to devise a common session which maximises benefit to all present. I have often handled three or more separate sessions simultaneously although obviously may have not been able to devote much attention to any one session or any one athlete. Typical groups would be 800/1500 (high speed), 5k/10k and upwards, and possibly newcomers or athletes coming back from injury. Where possible for each event range I devise one distance and recovery, with variations to accommodate as many athletes as possible. The athletes then work on their own. A major benefit to all the athletes stems from the group therapy, i.e. each athlete finds comfort from the fact that other athletes are working just as hard as he/she is, and usually suffering as much.

Sometimes the relationship with the coach is intense and the coach tends to seep into the mind of the athlete and vice versa. At Christmas 1992, five years after I moved north, I received a card from one athlete, in which he wrote," I still hear you shouting at me in the sessions." Many of the athletes I worked with did not fulfil their potential as a runner because of circumstances—but that is often the way of the world. However I still have feelings of guilt about some of them. Where did I go wrong? Each should have done better.

I have been lucky because as one athlete moved away from the group another joined the group. At the start of the Jogging Boom (See Chapter 8), Peter, a talented 800 metre runner, eased out of Athletics and along came Brian a 5ft 6in 29 year old ex-footballer, pulled into running on the jogging boom, "to run marathons", he later told me. Some basic speed, his natural tenacity, ferocious competitive instincts and an inability to run long distances without injury turned him towards 800 metre running. I learned much later when speaking to one of his school friends that Brian had been the fastest sprinter at school. He had been invited by a sprints coach to the track for sprint training and had been asked to sprint up and down the track all evening by the coach (who I never met). Brian's comments after that painful session were, "If that was running I didn't want to know." From 1983 to 1988 his 800 metre time improved yearly from 2m 05s to 1m 54.1s and in 1989 he ran 1m 54.3s.

Later I was asked to work with a talented 14 year old, whose coach at the time had stopped coaching. I had seen the athlete him around since he was 11 and knew him to be a talented runner. I was uneasy about the threat to my coaching reputation. If he did well it would be because of his talent. If he did badly it would be my fault. He and his mother came round to my house for a chat and he and I started to work together then. In the first few weeks I analysed his running action before allowing him to move into more intensive work. He was small and I asked him for weekly measurements of height and weight and at times modified sessions dependent on his recent growth rate. His previous coach had allowed him to take part in a 5000 metres so I had no objection to his running one in 1986 which he completed in an unstressed 16m 54s. He was an exceptional talent. During 1987 he improved, totally under control from 800 metres to 1500 metes.

In November 1987 following my move to Barrow-in-Furness in Cumbria I teamed up with Pat a 5' 11" fitter with a major shipbuilding employer in the town, for whom I also worked. Pat was 20 and came forward when I offered my services in coaching steeplechase. From initial analysis it was obvious that he was talented together with an intense desire to improve. In addition he had an unusual symmetry in range of movement and a highly developed spatial awareness, i.e. the sense of knowing where his limbs were in complex movements like hurdling. Prior to my arrival his best 800 metre time was 1m 58s. He had not run a steeplechase. He improved yearly over the next nine years to 8m 57.4s in the heats of AAA Champs in 1996. He now (2011) coaches a talented and enthusiastic group of young runners in Barrow.

In July 1997 my attention was drawn to a talented 14 year old boy, just under 6 feet tall, who lived just around the corner from me. He had run 2m 06s that year and was running in the English Schools 800 two weeks later. His father worked with a running friend of mine and discussed his son's aptitude for running and this resulted in him bringing his son to me. I asked the lad to walk up the road and sprint back to me between two lamp posts as fast as he could. As I watched him running the hairs on the back of my neck stood up. The talent was obvious and I asked him to repeat the sprint. I realised then that there were problems with the way he ran and he would need lots of correction. It worked in 2000 he was selected to run for England in the U18 age group over 800 metres. Following injuries in 2001 he set an early season 1m 51.7s in but then decided he did not then wish to continue his Athletic career. I felt saddened that a supreme talent of potential benefit to him and the country has been lost. Like so many athletes, he went to university and improved for a while, but finally disappeared from the results.

## 11. Improving Years on Year

Politicians regularly set targets which are dictated by political requirements and which are often impossible to achieve because they have not considered the resources needed to do the job. It is easy for coaches to do the same. When an athlete goes well and sets a personal best (pb) time, he looks so relaxed, some young athletes look adult, and it is easy for the coach to believe that there is much more "in the tank" and to set a programme which is too demanding for the current state of the athlete. How can this be avoided and year-on-year improvement sustained? One answer is to look at what improvement has been achieved in the past by other athletes, regardless of reasons. I have analysed results obtained from published ranking lists and from my own records for athletes coached by myself over a period of 4 or 5 years. I was unable to perform a rigorous mathematical analysis on the figures but argue that for practical purposes we can use annual improvements of between 1.5 and 2% of an event time as a practical annual target. However in exceptional cases, such as the two young 800 metre runners mentioned, their improvement of 12 seconds over three years was about 3% per year, which must be considered highly desirable, but unrealistic for most.

My view is that any programme should be ability-pushed rather than expectation-pulled. The programme must start at what the athlete can achieve now rather than what the coach thinks he should achieve. This reduces the probability of injury. At worst an annual improvement of 1.5 to 2% can be used. If this becomes too easy and the performance-pushed approach is used the target can be moved as the athlete progresses. This avoids the dangers of too high a target being set, with inevitable recriminations and loss of confidence on the part of the athlete. The content of each session will be dependent on the target event and realistic improvement on previous bests and can include excursions to other linked events, such as 400 or 1500m orientation for an 800 metre runner.

The main principles involved are as follows:

1.  Build on the strengths of the athlete. With the veteran athlete mentioned previously, his obvious strength was his disciplined approach

high regular mileage, which enabled him to run bulk sessions in which we could introduce faster running speeds than steady race pace, with confidence that he could achieve them.

2. Include favourite sessions regularly, if only because this heightens enjoyment for the athlete, the sole reason for his being in Athletics. However ensure that they are meaningful. For instance if he likes to run 10 x 200m with 200 jog, include such sessions as both reward and motivation.

3. Include sessions, which are necessary for improvement, even though the athlete may be uncomfortable. If he favours aerobic sessions, introduce anaerobic elements and vice versa.

4. Include test sessions or races in the programme to monitor progress and to provide feedback to the athlete. Praise the athlete if results are good, but also but be prepared to console him and pick him up if they are bad.

5. After the season, whether or not the target has been achieved, detailed and honest analysis should be conducted between the athlete and coach and then the next target should be discussed.

## 12. An Unexpected Benefit from Coaching

The world is an uncertain place and every so often a chance happening can result in changing your life completely. In 1987, when I was approaching a redundancy from a local company without another job to go to I had a coaching session at the track, one athlete being Dave, a steeplechaser. I had been coaching him for two years and the relationship had been beneficial. The session went well and we were both pleased with the results. We moved to the side of the track to the pile of clothing left by the athletes. He was the first to finish training and bent down, picked up his training top and started to pull it over his head. We discussed the results of his session and I complimented him on how he had done. He nodded, pleased at the session and also by my comments. "That was hard," he said, sweat pouring off his forehead. He sat down and started to pull his tracksuit bottoms over one foot, paused and looked at me.

"By the way," he said, "How's the job hunting?" "Oh, nothing's come up yet," I replied, "I've got another interview next week in London, but it's not very promising."

"What do you do, exactly?" he asked. "I'm a project engineer, manufacturing, testing, mainly in production." I replied.

"I'll tell you what," he said, "I was having a drink with my brother-in-law last night and he was moaning that he can't get any estimators around here and did I know of any? I told him "No, but I know one guy who's been around a bit. Could you do it, Barry?"

"Well. I'll try anything, I have to in my situation."

"OK then, I'll mention it to him when I see him next, I think it's next Thursday he's coming round."

The other athletes came back after their sessions, results were discussed, the athletes joked about the session and results and also the Athletics match the following Saturday. We then went our separate ways to our homes and I forgot the conversation with Dave before I got home. I presumed it had been just him being pleasant, a throwaway remark with no intent to do anything further about it.

The next night at about 10 o'clock the telephone rang. "Hello," I said quietly, wondering who it would be so late. It was Dave. "Hello Barry," he said, "I've talked to my brother-in-law about you and he wants to talk to you. Can you give him a ring at work tomorrow?"

"Yes, of course Dave, thanks a lot. I'll ring him. Give me the number." I wrote the number on pad of paper by the telephone.

I rang the number the next day, a large local engineering company and talked to the Personnel Department. We arranged to attend an interview with Dave's brother-in-law, Gary Jones. Fortunately I had a strong engineering background and also some financial knowledge so was able to give a good impression. After three interviews I was offered a job as a production planner/estimator, neither of which I had done before. Maybe they were as desperate as I was.

I threw myself energetically into the job, trying desperately to understand the product, the process and, most importantly, the costing implications. I did this well enough for me to be kept on past the probationary period. I felt I was doing all right and then some three months later we were informed that the company was to be taken over. The kick in the teeth came when we were told that the company was to be closed down within three months and I was one of those in the last phase of being made redundant, but was being given an extra month's pay as a bonus for staying to the end.

I intensified my attempts to obtain another job, replying to adverts from all the country and one day a plain brown A5 envelope dropped through our letter box, with a letter asking me to go to Barrow-in Furness, in Cumbria for an interview as a Project Engineer in a shipbuilding company. The first thing which my wife and I did was to look into our road map to find out where Barrow-in Furness was. At the interview, which was for a Project Engineer I was asked about my experience as an Estimator, which I had mentioned on the application form for the job. I was honest in my replies and answered their questions well and ultimately was offered a job as an Estimator and not as a Project Engineer. Apparently there was then a similar shortage of estimators in the Northwest as in Sussex.

The job offer came when I was working out my last week for the company before it was closed down. That conversation with Dave after his training resulted in my obtaining a few months experience as an estimator and this opened up employment opportunities in a Commercial departments for a further five years, although many miles away. My estimating experience had lasted some three months. It turned out that the company in Cumbria had been unsuccessful in obtaining any applicants for their estimating departments, probably because of the location of the company, miles from any major towns. After staying an extra day for further interviews I was offered and accepted a job as a Senior Estimator and started there just one week after being made redundant from the previous company, where I had been for only six months.

That training session, in which David was feeling good because of his training results and his desire to help me, resulted in my starting another job in Cumbria in November 1987, which lasted for nearly four years. Soon afterwards going to Barrow I joined Barrow & Furness Striders Athletic Club and started coaching runners there.

## 13. An Unusual Older Athlete Coaching Assignment

In "The Jogging Boom" in Chapter 8 I stated that many joggers, some approaching middle age, became successful club runners later in their careers, some of them flourishing in the 800 and 1500 metre region, where leg speed becomes important. It seemed as though this leg speed would have been nourished faster if they had received tuition early in their lives. Their increased running speed had waited until the point in their lives when they had started for the first time to receive a programme aimed at enabling them to run faster. I believe that this retention of capability resides in the body for many years.

I was able to test this theory when I received a telephone call in May 2009 from Richard Walker, then 35 years old, who I had met and coached in 1990. He was then a talented 16 year old and finished in the low twenties in the National U17 Cross Country Championships. In addition, in that year at the end of a rigorous Young Athlete's coaching session he ran a 1500 metre steeplechase time trial in 4min 40.1secs, the equivalent same time for the one mile flat. For a while he improved and then, like so many young people, drifted away from Athletics. From time to time we would meet and chat about "Running" until in 2005 I moved to Horsham in West Sussex.

After his telephone call I prepared a twelve-week programme for him, recognising that he was nearly 20 years older than when we had last worked together as a coach-athlete team. I applied my standard "New athlete" approach, as follows:

1. Establish the athlete's present fitness level.
2. Prepare an improvement programme.
3. Implement the programme.

I knew that before contacting me he had been running regularly, so I could assume some level of fitness. The first significant restriction I faced was that I could not ask him to perform the high intensity drills and sprint sessions, which would have been applicable when he was younger, if only because his physiology would not be able to withstand the forces involved and injury would result. This reasoning pointed towards a programme based on his strengths, which were primarily high level of aerobic endurance, i.e. he was a good runner. I knew that he had been very competitive and relied on this, hoping that this feature could be utilised in obtaining improvement in running speed. It was essential to keep his mileage low initially and to increase leg speed before increase mileage. This was fundamentally because increase in mileage is invariably accompanied by reduction in leg speed.

I set a programme which required him to continue running as he had been, but, included one session per week aimed at starting him on the road to running faster. I had used these sessions with numbers of athletes over the years both in the North of England and later in the south after my move and knew that they worked.

Richard used the latest technology in recording training and racing times. I was able to monitor his progress regularly over the internet, using daily mileage, times recorded in specific sessions and telephone calls between us as my major information sources. These specific sessions were primarily bulk, off short recoveries and I required one specific on steady state running session per week. Typical sessions were 8 x 800 metres (session distance 6.4k), or 6 x 1k (session distance 6k), or 5 x 1200 metres (session distance 6k) on the road with 90 seconds walk (static) recovery between runs. These sessions would stretch him aerobically but should not affect his leg speed. The muscle-stretch phenomena induced by each session would stay in his system for well over a week so it was possible to use the stretch-effects of one week's session as an introduction to that of the next week.

Each session utilised that of the previous week and it was possible to move him up-distance with longer repetition long runs off the same short recovery. These sessions were useful in simulating race conditions and are possibly what is meant by that much-used term "Tempo" run, although I have not seen it defined and assume that it means running at a high intensity. A standard test session, usually 8 x 800 with 90 seconds recovery was used regularly as a test session at the end of each 12-week period to provide useful performance-related data. There is an interesting and repeatable correlation between the average times run by an athlete in this test session and the times run in races.

I recommend that the minimum distance used for older endurance athletes should be 200 metres. This distance is multi-faceted because it can be used for absolute speed, or in bulk as a high-calibre endurance workout. A typical session would be 5 sets of 800/200 metres, with recovery 90 seconds, total session distance being 5000 metres. Recoveries before and after the 200's can be varied but with compensating changes in the recoveries.

The athlete is regularly in contact with other athletes and sometimes feels that he would like to run in a particular race, without considering if his training is sufficient. It may be that his friends are going, he just feels like trying it, especially if the race has been popular over the years. In Cumbria such as race is the Coniston 14, a 14 plus mile circuit around Coniston Water. Richard mentioned the forthcoming race to me and of his desire to run it and I advised him strongly not to run it because he had not run enough miles in training and I knew that problems would occur in the last part of the race, for which the runner needs many miles in preparation. Despite my advice he ran the race and finished 4th, driven by his intense competitive instincts and self-drive. Unfortunately for him the race that year had been extended by two miles up to over sixteen miles and the effort he expended brought on respiratory problems for about a year. That problem has now been overcome and earlier this year (2011) he ran his fastest 5k on the road since his comeback. When we met I was able to let him know precisely what I felt of his decision, using very strong (for me) language and he took it on the chin.

Now we must move forward, his main target being to improve and to be as fast as possible for his entry in to the veteran ranks (over 40) for men in May 2014. I look upon it as an absorbing challenge. As has been said as we get older we get slower. Each of us has hidden characteristics, which may be harnessed and the ageing process may be held at bay for a while. My job is to prepare a programme to enable him to run faster than ever before, over 10k. His current form suggests that he can run between 33 and 34 minutes for 10k now and I will use my often-stated principle that the most important session for an athlete is the next one. I have to ensure that each session takes him a little further along the improvement road. His task is to perform the sessions. Either of us could be sidelined by illness or injury. He might get there but how fast will he run? The answer depends primarily on freedom from injury or injury and then doing the doing the training. If the balance of the sessions and mileage is correct I believe that a he can run between 31 to 32 minutes 10k in May 2014.

END

# CHAPTER 13

# OLDER AND SLOWER

One of the absolutes in life is that we slow down as we get older because most physiological and anatomical processes degrade with age. Some aggressive people believe that this does not apply to them and say things like, "I'm as strong, good, hard, etc, as I was ten years ago". Alas he or she is deluding him/herself. Throughout history there have been constant searches for the elixir for eternal youth and this century is no exception. Fortunes have been spent by people and multi-national organisations on beauty and fitness products to continue this quest.

One partially successful path, which leads to a rejuvenation of sorts, can be found in maintaining the body at a high physical fitness level. In my case and with many others love of running and continued drive for improvement has enabled me to maintain a very efficient cardio-vascular system, that wonderful combination within the body of two pumps working in harness, the lungs and heart, which provide a plentiful supply of oxygen to the limbs and removal of waste products from the muscles through the heart and lungs to the atmosphere. I believe that major benefits result from improved physical fitness, primarily because the improved blood supply contains substances, which help in healing injuries and tissue damage, and also give short-term feel-good periods, although usually these are followed by aches in all sorts of places.

In the last twenty years in the 1990's and in the noughties there has been a growth of veteran running, or runners continuing the training they had done since they started to run many years before. In addition in what has been a fun, or social running boom many older people have taken up running, attracted by the city marathons and other distances.

For every athlete at any time of year, if we could measure the worth of every training run or race, we would find that performance moves up and down, rather like the stock market index of a share. These changes occur for a number of reasons, variation in intensity of training, illness, injury, work or domestic pressure, etc. When training stops, performance will be maintained for a short period (of days) before gradually dropping off. The athlete should not be unduly alarmed if he catches a cold or virus, unless it stays for longer than a week, after which time performance would be expected to decline. This phenomenon is called the "Droop" effect.

## Personal Times over a number of years

The overall trend as one gets older is for running speed to slow, and for performances to drop off, although for number of years performance stays sensibly the same,

Barry Worrall·

governed purely by training and competition. I have
always welcomed the approach of the cross-country
season and my personal indicator of its start was the
Reigate Priory Relays, held for many years on the first
Saturday in November. Each team was composed of six
runners and each ran the same course. I ran this race
over the same 2.75-mile course for Crawley AC from
1972 to 1986, before the hurricane in September of
1987 brought down many trees and caused the course
to be changed for many years. It is now run over the
original course. From 1972 to 1986, the period under
review, my training diaries show that I averaged 30/35
miles per week, on 5/6 days per week, a low mileage
runner by any standards. My times achieved in that
period are shown in Table 1 below:

TABLE 1: REIGATE PRIORY RELAYS—RUNNING TIMES

| YEAR | TIME | YEAR | TIME | YEAR | TIME | YEAR | TIME |
|------|------|------|------|------|------|------|------|
| 1972 | 15m 04s | 1976 | Injured | 1980 | 15m 44s | 1984 | 16m 01s |
| 1973 | 15m 29s | 1977 | 15m 16s | 1981 | 15m 46s | 1985 | 18m 10s |
| 1974 | 15m 48s | 1978 | Injured | 1982 | Injured | 1986 | 17m 24s |
| 1975** | 15m 21s | 1979 | 15m 11s | 1983 | 16m 16s | | |

** First year as a Veteran aged 40.

It appears that as I got older I was able to run roughly
the same time for a few years, but if there was a break
I would return with slower times, which would be
maintained until the next break. I suspect that this
trend will occur with other athletes.

In the sixties, seventies and eighties running was
popular in this country. The Area and National

Championships Cross Country Championships were "Eyeballs out" by most competitors, from the fast front men to the slower people in the middle and back. In the main championships the oldest competitive levels were Seniors, Juniors and Youths for men and similar age groups for women. The veterans (over 40 for men, over 35 for women) had their own championships. As time passed, it was found that fewer younger runners were appearing. In many road races the average age of runners has increased. It may be that the veterans wished to maintain their fitness and enjoyed the racing and camaraderie. Coupled with this has been the growth for the younger generation of computer games, and a drift away from intense exercises, couple with increased leisure activities available, the trend towards comfort foods and lifestyles etc. Veteran's athletics took off and there was an added spice in training because you could then compete against people and get away from those younger, harder and faster runners. Then in the early eighties came the phenomenon that many competitors in road races around the country were veterans and now, in 2011, the majority of runners in road races are veterans. It appears that younger runners are not competing in these events.

The main trend for any runner is that running performance, like all physiological processes, usually degrades with increasing age. This process can be temporarily halted by changes in training regime and possibly by new sessions suited to your performance, life style, weight, etc. However, by the time you reach middle age, your body will have become accustomed to your habits and will have started the process of slowing down.

## Practical sessions for older athletes

In 2005 my wife and I moved back from Cumbria and I started to coach a small group of three men and one woman, all in their forties. in Horsham. My approach to each was exactly the same as with any other athlete, as stated in the last chapter, but repeated here for convenience:

1. Establish the initial fitness level
2. Determine an improvement programme
3. Implement the programme

In the Sussex Veterans' Cross Country Championships in Horsham in December 2007 one of them, a 49 year old male athlete finished 18th in the Over 40 race, six positions higher up than the previous year, but 28 seconds slower, with underfoot conditions much worse. Such improvement with increasing age is unusual. I treated these athletes no differently to any other athlete and with each, established their individual starting points, dictated by their individual fitness, strength. weaknesses, ambition and physical state. Veteran runners have usually been running for a long time and are highly motivated and strong runners, even if steady paced and each exhibited a strong desire to improve. Their weaknesses were quite simply that each had been subjected to the body's ageing physiological and anatomical processes, i.e. they had been getting older. In this case joints and limbs cannot be subjected to the severe anaerobic processes and power applications deemed suitable for younger athletes. Most older athletes are reluctant to accept this limitation and are prone to over-use injuries by attempting sessions more suitable for younger athletes.

The athletes in this group all had busy lives as professional people and time spent in training was grudgingly given and weekly mileage was low by most standards, say 30 to 40 miles per week off four to five days per week. Somehow each managed to allocate time to train within their family, social and professional lives. After an initial discussion with each to establish a starting point well within their individual capabilities I asked each to perform a simple session on the track 8 x 400 metres on the track with 100 metres jog recovery on their own and this became the norm for the sessions, even when other athletes were present. It was essential for each athlete to understand his/her own pace and not be caught up in a competitive sessions with other athletes. In every non-steady-state session this practice was maintained. The session in each week was different to the previous one and slightly more demanding or difficult. Session content was changed weekly and progressively until after say six weeks when a session was repeated there was in each case a noticeable improvement. It takes a number of sessions before each athlete masters the required mental processes and then session content can be varied to make successive sessions more demanding. A typical and successful programme sequence, using one session per week, with a constant 90 seconds recovery is as follows:

8 x 800, 6 x 1000, 5 x 1200, 6 x 1000, 8 x 800.

It will be noticed that these sessions are similar to those used with the joggers as shown in chapter 8. The variation in distances from one week's session to another was deliberate on my part, because of results from similar sessions with athletes in the past. Times of the last session can be compared with those of the first. An additional session uses a shallow hill, about 150 metres long up which the athlete runs hard and then jogs back down. Time for the uphill should be 30 seconds or so and the time for the jog down should be 90 seconds maximum. This session forces the athlete onto the balls of the feet, to push off on the toes and enforces improved running technique. An additional benefit is that the athlete runs against body weight and the session becomes resistive. Significant and constant improvement in running speed can be obtained if the hill sessions are alternated weekly with the above bulk short recovery sessions.

## Safety in Running

As has been stated, with every step the runner pushes into the ground with a force equal to between two and five times body weight and the ground effectively pushes back. There is therefore a risk with every step of causing an injury of one sort or another and this risk increases with age. Fortunately with human locomotion such injuries are rare but they do happen. Most runners will fall over at sometime in their career, possibly from a slippery surface, a tree root in cross country forest runs, a stone kerb, uneven pavements, etc. Mostly they get up and continue to run, although a little shaken and with no long-term ill effects. In all probability the runner does not know precisely where he will plant the foot and continue over the ground.

However with increasing age balance starts to degrade and the older athlete should try to focus on safety aspects of any run, in particular on the precise spot on which the foot will land. Many councils delay repairing roads and pavements, which can become dangerous because of deep potholes. My own practice is to focus on the pavement, road or track in the twenty metres or so immediately in front of me. In addition major hazards to runners occur at roundabouts, primarily because of slipshod use by motorists of the use of signals on leaving the roundabouts. My own experience and estimate on local roundabouts is that about 10% of drivers indicate wrongly and are potentially lethal to a runner wanting to cross one of the roads close to the roundabouts. Ideally the runner should monitor the line of drive of the car and should not cross a road until he is absolutely sure it is safe to do so. In such situations it is better to trust one's ears and eyes for engine noises and line of drive. The runner should always check with a glance behind and in front before crossing any junction—simple, but necessary. The many older runners seen on our roads is evidence that many people are coping well with advancing years.

END

# CHAPTER 14

## COE AND OVETT

At any time in any sport there are always a few performers who compete regularly among themselves for the top spots. They each have their supporters within that sport, some supporters being fanatical. This is the case in Athletics and each year fans look forward with keen anticipation to the competitions between their favourites and off track discussions between supporters of one or other of these athletes can continue well into the nights. Normally these intense discussions stay within the sport, but in the case of Ovett and Coe, the interest and following went outside these boundaries and into the living rooms of the UK and into the lives of the normally non-athletic-minded public. In writing about these two super-superstars of the running track I feel inadequate because of all that has been written about them by the best sports writers around. At best I can only present my personal view of them as it appeared at the time.

My view starts in Montreal on the St. Lawrence River in Quebec, Canada, to which city I moved in February 1967 as a minor element in the "Brain Drain", the recruitment of British engineers to North America (USA and the Canada) to work on the US space programme. Two and a half years later, in September 1969 my wife and I and our young family left Canada for Boston, Massachusets in the USA and in May 1971 we returned to England where I continued my Athletics career and where we have remained. Five years later, in 1976, my thoughts returned to Montreal because that city was the venue for that year's Olympic Games. They were as exciting as the Olympics always are and were watched avidly by me and a large part of the public in this country.

To me a major impact in the 800 metre was the presence of that speedy Cuban giant, Alberto Juantorena, (6 feet 3 inches (190cms) tall and weighing 185lbs (84kgs), who won an unusual (at Olympic Level) 400/800 metre double, the latter in a new world record of 1m 43.5s. Steve Ovett, then aged twenty and six feet tall, was our sole representative in that race, started in the outside lane round the first bend, seemed to move backwards throughout the race and finished fifth in 1m 45.4s. Coe was not selected for these Games. As I looked at Juantorena, with so much power and speed I felt that 800-metre running was at its peak and that no athlete would ever run faster. I had forgotten that a world record is only borrowed and that someone will come along and beat it. That someone was the (relatively) diminutive Seb Coe, 5 feet 9.5 inches (177 cms) tall and weighing only 123lbs (56kgs), in his first world record, 1m 42.4s, in 1979. The link between Juantorena and Coe was that Coe held the 800 metres world record (in 1979—with 1m 42.2s) and also 1981 (1m 41.73s). The link between Juantorena and Ovett was that the latter became the Olympic 800 metre champion, in the Moscow Games in 1980.

My links with Coe and Ovett continued when in October 1983 I passed the exams set by the Amateur Athletic Association (A.A.A.) and became a Senior Coach for 800/1500 and 5000/10000 metres. In the exam the main question was to state and discuss the strengths, weaknesses, achievements, training, etc., of the winners of the men's 800 and 1500 metres in the 1980 Moscow Olympics. The first and vital point to answer was, who were they and I knew this, along with every other athletics fan in the country. I cannot reproduce my answer here but I passed the exam so satisfied the examiners. Later I became a Senior Coach, Steeplechase.

Now we must step back in time to March 1972, in Hillingdon, Middlesex when the English Schools Intermediate Boys Cross Country Championships was won by 16 year old Kirk Dumpleton. In second place 200 metres behind, was S. Ovett, also 16 and in tenth place was S. Coe, then 15. Dumpleton went on to become a high calibre club runner and quietly slipped out of the spotlight while Ovett and Coe created their own world-media frenzy. Dumpleton is thought to be the only Englishman to beat in the same race these two special runners whose efforts played a large part in shaping the destiny of British 800 and 1500 metre running for a period of fifteen years or so from the mid 1970's to the late 1980's.

The Coe/Ovett confrontation period, in which they competed regularly on the track for GB ranged from 1976 to 1986, when Ovett's career started to wind down. Their last major Olympic presence was in the 1984 Games in Los Angeles. There Coe triumphed in the 1500 metres and became the only man in history to retain the 1500 metre title. My great sadness in those Games arose from Steve Ovett's breathing problems which manifested themselves in the 800 metre heats and resulted in him withdrawing from the 1500. If only he had elected to run just the 1500, there may have been a different result, because of his proven experience and ability at that distance. The heats of the 800's, each more ferocious than the previous, would have torn to shreds his strength reserves required to run the 1500's, his probable optimum distance. However history is full of "What if's" and we must accept reality.

In this fifteen year period there were of course other superb athletes who competed ferociously over the 800/1500 metre distances, namely Steve Cramm, Peter Elliot, and others who excelled at Olympic and world levels.

**Public Interest**

I have two examples of this public interest in Coe and Ovett. In July 1991, my wife and I were on holiday in Portpatrick, a small but beautiful harbour on the extreme west coast of Galloway in Scotland, just 26 miles or so from Ireland, the closest these countries come. We had gone there to visit a particular restaurant situated in the middle of the very short harbour, because of the reported high quality cuisine. We went into the restaurant, sat down at a vacant table and ordered our meal. Shortly afterwards we were joined by another couple who asked if they could occupy the two vacant chairs and of course we nodded cheerfully. We chatted across the table and got on well. As usual on such occasions subjects soon went to what you do for a living and sport.

Soon my enthusiasm for Athletics became evident and also the fact that I was a runner. When we mentioned that we were from Sussex, the man asked if I knew Steve Ovett and I nodded because I had seen him regularly in Sussex races, and of course on TV. The man and his wife became excited at the news and for some time we talked about Coe and Ovett. I assume that in these discussions I would have monopolised the conversation on that topic, discussed regularly on my Thursday nights out with my athletics friends. The food, service and conversation made a lasting impression on us. After a delightful evening the man told us of a very well-known seafood restaurant in Ullapool, a long way upon the west coast. Following his recommendations the next day we drove up to Ullapool where we stayed two nights in our tent on the local camp site. That restaurant lived up to its reputation. We visited Ullapool a few years later so our recollection of the visit and the restaurant was once again a priority-eating place for us.

Much later, in July 2010 I went to the public library in Horsham to obtain, "The Perfect Distance" a definitive account of the Coe/Ovett rivalry, written by Pat Butcher. The book has on its front cover a black and white photograph of them at the start of the final straight in the 1980 Moscow Olympic 800 metre final, which, of course Ovett won (some people say Coe lost that race). I handed the book over to the lady librarian for passing through the scanner. She glanced down at the book cover, paused, looked up at me and her face broke out into a smile. "Oh, I did so enjoy watching them on TV," she said. She was of course talking about events which had taken place nearly thirty years previously, but she remembered them with affection.

These two athletes (and of course others) thrilled the TV audiences during this fifteen year period and were in their own turn, overtaken by other athletes, from many countries. Those of us in the Sport knew that this dominance could not last and many coaches from around the world came to the UK to find out how we did it. Many contacted the British Milers Club (BMC) whose efforts played a major part in the renaissance of middle-distance running in this country. As always, in any technology and human activity, those who wish to improve look to the best in the world and try to emulate them, using their techniques. In my opinion, they were bound to fail if they were searching for a formula, because there wasn't one. In my view the domination of British middle distance running was due to several two-person coach/athlete teams and the methods of each coach were different, but they worked with the specific athletes.

The mantle of the best runners in the world has shifted from country to country since the early twentieth century and has accelerated since the Second World

War. Nowadays (2011) this rests firmly with the African nations, Kenya and Ethiopia, but their athletes will be beaten in their turn by faster and tougher men on the day. However back to Coe and Ovett, whose exploits thrilled the TV-watching public.

The 800 and 1500 metre races in the 1980 Olympics in Moscow provided defining moments for the public if only because both Coe and Ovett each won the other's specialist event. The media love to create an air of conflict between the sports people who top any sport but rarely does it really exist between the principals. Going into the Moscow Olympics Coe held the world record for 800 metres and Ovett had not lost a 1500 metre race for many months. Conventional thinking (to which I subscribed) is that Coe lost the 800 by going straight to the back of the field on the first lap and not appreciating, particularly in the 800 metres, that it is very difficult to accelerate from a fast pace. In the 1500 final, which took place a few days later Ovett was expected to win (and I agreed with this thinking) because of his long record in winning 1500's. He may have been confident in beating Coe in that final but he could not have anticipated Coe's ferocious determination to eliminate his 800-metre failure (in his eyes) from the records. Confrontations between the best are often decided by very small margins of accuracy and timing, whilst under intense pressure, i.e. by the athlete with the stronger desire to win.

My personal memories of Ovett, seen often at Crystal Palace, were of his seeming physical nonchalance and possibly, physical arrogance. In the 1500's he would sit in the pack until just before the 200 metres-to-go mark. He would casually look round and then within ten strides he had established a lead around the final bend, two metres, then three and up to ten metres in the final straight, along which he would look up into the packed main stand and wave with his right hand, at the same time, grinning cheekily. And the crowd loved it.

Apart from some major championships at Crystal Palace I did not see Coe much in the flesh and was amazed by his ability to maintain high knee lift and leg speed in the last 150 metres of an 800 or1000 metres. I saw him once running a leg (I think for Belgrave Harriers) in a Southern 12 man road relay and was given a demonstration of an athlete exerting maximum and obviously painful effort in his running. And he was an 800-metre runner. These examples suggest that the requirements of a top-level 800-metre runner are primarily very high speed-capability and the strength in body and mind to drive him/herself to and beyond the limits of human activity. The requirements of any 800/1500m runner wanting to be the best at 800 metres is that he should be able to take on and compete well and sometimes beat the up-distance runners at their own distances.

These memories are of course personal and I have not been able to mention many other fine athletes and in my coaching I have tried to enthuse my athletes with the imagery of these two special athletes. Within that fifteen-year period highly talented foreign athletes were unlucky because in most major Games they would finish behind one or other of British runners who dominated the 800/1500 metre region, including the mile, the historical classic race.

# CHAPTER 15

# OLYMPIC PROSPECTS—2012

In August 2012 the eyes of the country, and indeed the World, will be focused on London and primarily onto the Olympic Stadium in Stratford. I have always welcomed the approach of any major championships in Athletics with excitement and hope, excitement because of the quality of the performances to be set up and the hope that our own country will do well. There is always drama when the best take on the best. Like all sports and much else Athletics has changed dramatically since I was a spectator at the 1960 Olympics in Rome but some things stay the same.

There will be political interference and governments of some countries will attempt to sabotage the Games, if only to prevent their athletes from coming into contact with athletes of their own age with political or religious beliefs contrary to their own. For the London Games and probably for all future Games and similar world wide sporting occasions the temptation to take advantage of the attendance of the world's media will be overwhelming for terrorist or fanatical groups of various kinds. Security considerations and costs will therefore be high. The overall costs of staging these Games will be high and contentious but in my view it is essential that they continue and the dark forces of evil and destruction do not succeed. I have always resisted political dominance of sporting occasions because the politicians will always have different agendas to those of the sporting bodies and of the participating athletes. Boycotts will continue but inevitably they fail because they deny the athletes (citizens) of the boycotting country the opportunity to meet their counterparts in other countries. The world is shrinking and sporting occasions, like Mao Tse Tung's "politics" are "War without the fighting." It is for each individual to make up his or her own mind whether to compete or not.

There will be surprises, some good for us, some bad. The eyes of the world will be on the Athletics Arena for the best part of 10 days, I believe that runners (events from 800 metres upwards) from Great Britain will be scarce in the finals (or the best eight in the world) because of the way in which our standards have fallen well behind those of the rest of the world. As a coach I feel responsible in some way, although do not know what I could have done differently to change this outcome.

## Declining Running Standards—Western World

Using data obtained from published results, I have analysed details of one event, the men's 800 metres winners in Olympic Games from 1972 to 2008 and of the highest ranked GB athletes since 2001. I feel that the picture shown for this event will be constant across other running events, from 1500 metres to marathon. These selections are personal, arbitrary and open to criticism but they provide some useful data. In the men's 800 metres, from 1972 to 2008 there has been one British winner, namely Steve Ovett in Moscow in 1980. In the women's 800 there has been one winner, Kelly Holmes in Athens in 2008. Over this 36-year period the average age of the men winners was 23 and the average winning time was 1 minute 44.0 seconds. For British runners since 2001, chosen to show probable current standards, the average season's best performance time has been 1minute 45.41 seconds, with the same average age of 23. It is said that "There are lies, damned lies and statistics", but I am comfortable with predicting that the winning time for men in 2012 will be 1m 44.0s and the winner will be 23 years old, or 22 now (in 2011). In 2011 the fastest British men's 800 metre time was Michael Rimmer's 1m 43.89s and he has about six months to become a major contender for the final of the 800 metres. However a faster time, probably to the 1m 42.0 region, will be needed in to win the 800 because the athlete will then be required to race in the qualifying rounds, probably five races in all, with each round getting tougher and faster. This is not impossible in his case. With the other running events a similar situation prevails.

The situation regarding the women is better, but not by much. The British women's performances are better in world terms than those of the men, but podium spots (or top three) are unlikely. Success in the distance running events (from 800 metres to marathon) depends on someone finding ways of obtaining improvements over the next 12 months which have rarely been achieved without the use of drugs or banned substances and the athlete must be already visible on the athletic circuit. In my view this is unlikely, but miracles can happen. Another probable hindrance to any likely candidate will be media attention, because of their desperate need of sporting heroes or heroines.

Why is success in the running events so important? Simply because these events take longer to complete than the sprints and in each race the crowd becomes involved with the progress of a race and public morale is served well and improved (as all politicians know) if home athletes are in with a chance. Despite the above pessimistic forecast it is necessary to research ways in which an athlete can do enough work in sessions and build in sufficient recovery, stretch tissues and oxygen transport to be strong enough to beat the best runners in the world, at present mainly African.

## The Athlete's Life

Accepting that the winning athlete will now be aged 22 (23 in 2012) the next 8 months or so will find him training and racing ferociously at his event while, if he is in employment at the same time going through the process of earning a living, studying, industrial training or in a full time job. He must learn to separate elements of his life into compartments, in each one being able to focus totally on the needs of that compartment. Lottery funding will assist some of these athletes but some will be able to work or study to finance their life styles, academic, employment, pleasure-seeking and sporting.

Those on lottery funding will need to conform to the restraints and regular auditing from the bureaucratic and accountant-driven lottery funding system operated by Athletics UK. This will almost certainly be performance-driven. Those lucky people who can combine an industrial or other paid employment with an athletics career will be able to reduce this interference in their lives and will have larger degrees of freedom. However they must rigorously search their days to find time to train to the necessary intensity. It will not easy but is just possible within the current timescale. We may do better in some non-running events, the sprints and hurdles. However I agree with selection on a results-oriented basis and for those selected appropriate coaching resources should be provided.

We are in an era of funding for success and the Olympics themselves will be a success because lottery funding will be provided to those sports which can almost guarantee medals such as, the sitting down sports, cycling, equestrianism, sculling, yachting, etc. With regard to Athletics we may have to rely on the preserve of the maverick coach/athlete teams. We shall see.

END

# ACKNOWLEDGEMENTS AND REFERENCES

## Publications used for references in this book are as follows:

### Athletics Magazines

Athletics Weekly—dates from 1970 to 2011
International Track and Field Manual—various
Athletics Monthly—various

### Books

Training Distance Runners—David Martin & Peter Coe
Rules For Competition—British Athletics Federation
The Sony Guide To Who's Who in The 1984 Olympics—Pelham Books
Principles of Anatomy and Physiology—Tortora and Anagnostakos
And many others

### Writing Conventions

In Athletics the methods of denoting distances and times are various, as follows:

## 1. Distances

Usually race distances are denoted by 'm' for metres, 'k' or 'km' for kilometres.

## 2. Times

Where a time is used in conversation or in text the words are spelt out in full. Eg: a four minute mile. Times shown during races are in the format ?h ?m ?s where h denotes hours, n denotes minutes and s denotes seconds. Other expressions are 'min' for minutes, 'sec' for seconds. Times recorded by the author are taken from his own records. World and other records and venues are taken from the Athletics media.

## Errors

The author apologises in advance for any errors which may remain in the text despite rigorous checking. He asks the reader to inform him of any such errors.